LiZZiE M^cGUiRE

Volume 10

Series created by Terri Minsky

Best Dressed for Much Less

written by Bob Thomas

Inner Beauty

written by Melissa Gould

Editor - Erin Stein
Contributing Editor - Marian Brown
Graphic Designer and Letterer - Monalisa J. de Asis
Cover Designer - Patrick Hook

Digital Imaging Manager - Chris Buford
Pre-Press Manager - Antonio DePietro
Production Managers - Jennifer Miller and Mutsumi Miyazaki
Art Director - Matt Alford
Senior Editor - Elizabeth Hurchalla
Managing Editor - Jill Freshney
VP of Production - Ron Klamert
President & C.O.O. - John Parker
Publisher & C.E.O. - Stuart Levy

E-mail: info@tokyopop.com
Come visit us online at www.TOKYOPOP.com

A **TOKYOPOP** Cine-Manga® Book
TOKYOPOP Inc.
5900 Wilshire Blvd., Suite 2000
Los Angeles, CA 90036

Lizzie McGuire Volume 10

ISBN: 1-59532-281-7

First TOKYOPOP® printing: February 2005

10 9 8 7 6 5 4 3 2 1

Printed in China

Lizzie McGUiRE

Volume 10

CONTENTS

Lizzie McGuire

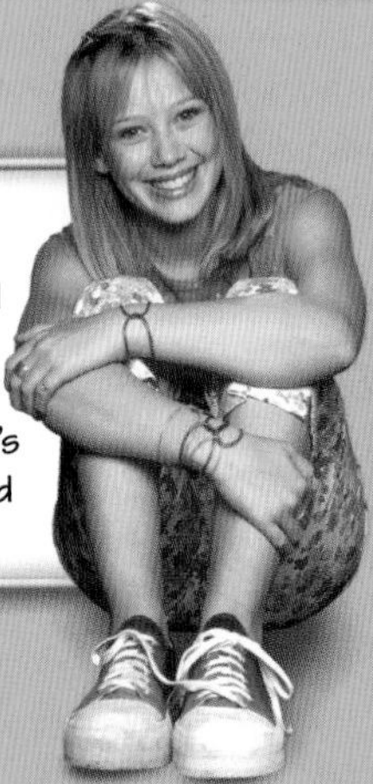

LIZZIE McGUIRE:
A typical 14-year-old girl who has her fair share of bad hair days and embarrassing moments. Luckily, Lizzie knows how to admit when she's wrong, back up her friends and stand up for herself.

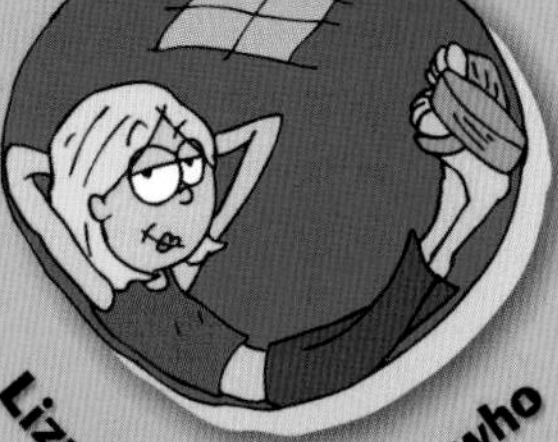

Lizzie's alter-ego, who says and does all the things Lizzie's afraid to.

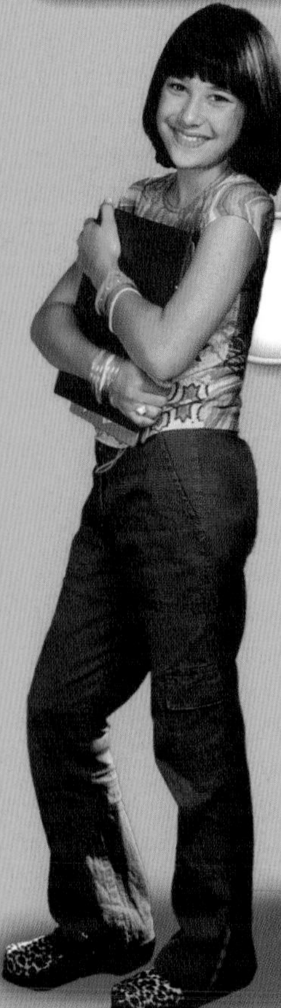

MIRANDA:
Lizzie's best friend.

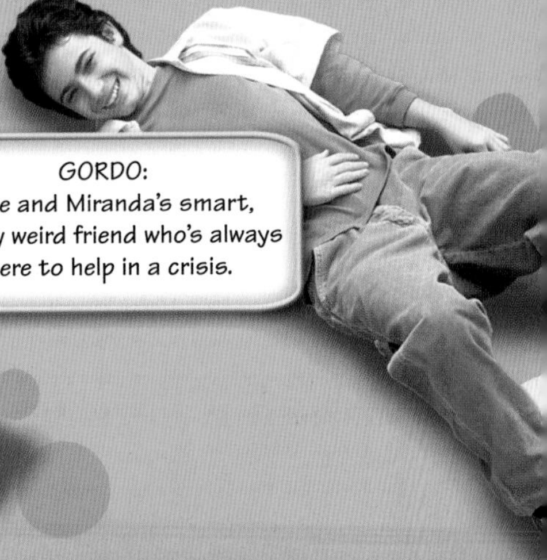

GORDO:
Lizzie and Miranda's smart, slightly weird friend who's always there to help in a crisis.

CHARACTER BIOS

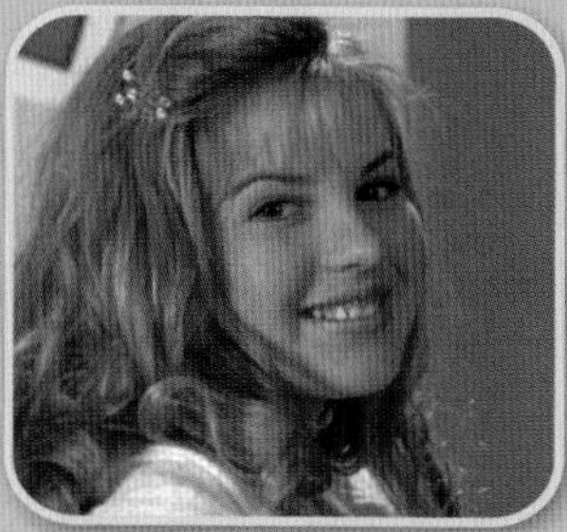

KATE:
Lizzie and Miranda's ex-friend who thinks she is too good for them now that she wears a bra.

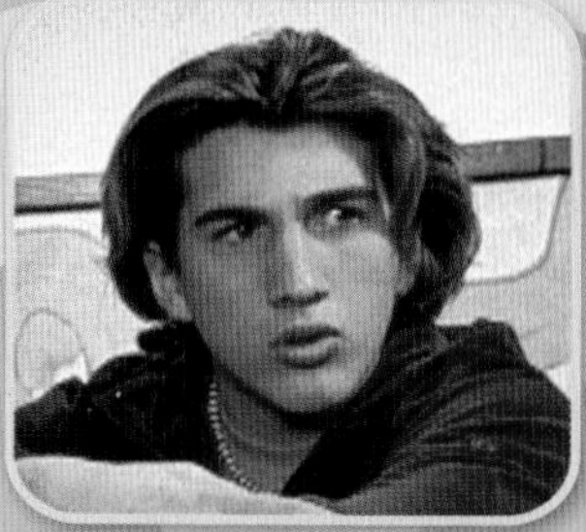

ETHAN:
The most popular guy in school.

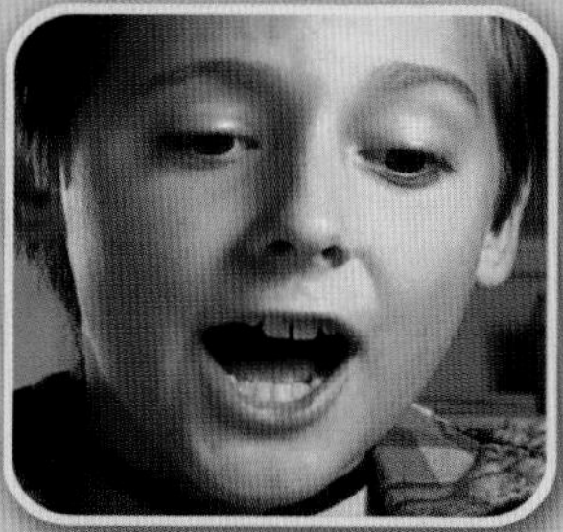

MATT:
Lizzie's little brother, who spends most of his time driving her crazy.

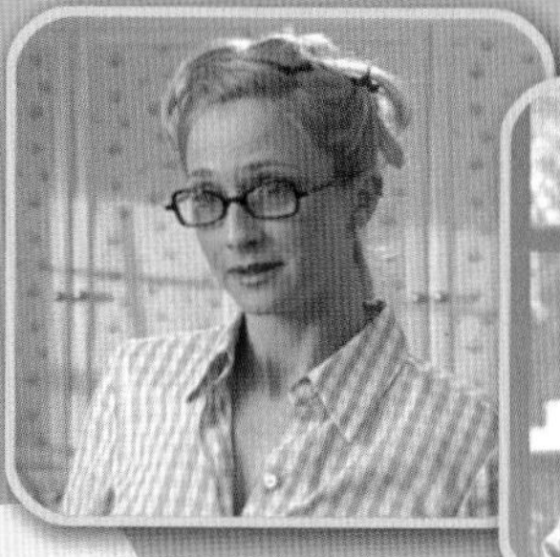

LIZZIE'S MOM:
She only wants the best for Lizzie, but sometimes she tries a little too hard.

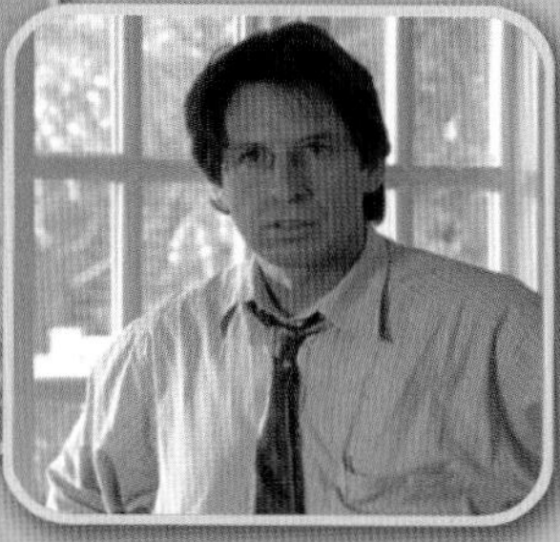

LIZZIE'S DAD:
He loves Lizzie, though he doesn't always know how to relate to her.

Lizzie McGuire

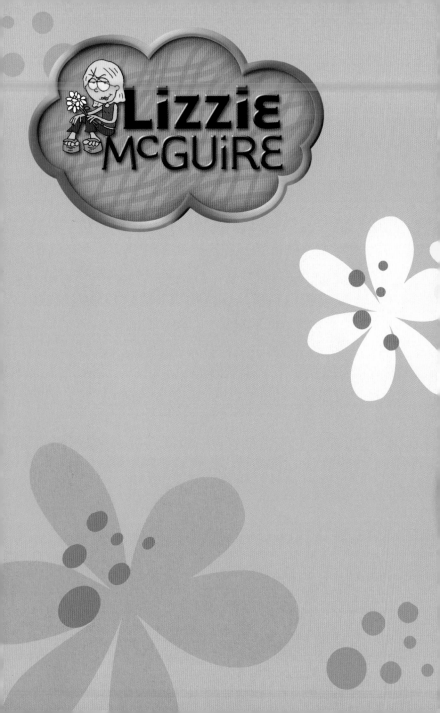

Best Dressed for Much Less

The school is voting for "Best Dressed" and Lizzie knows she can win if she can just get those awesome hip-huggers from the Style Shack. Her mom has other ideas, though, that involve bargain shopping!

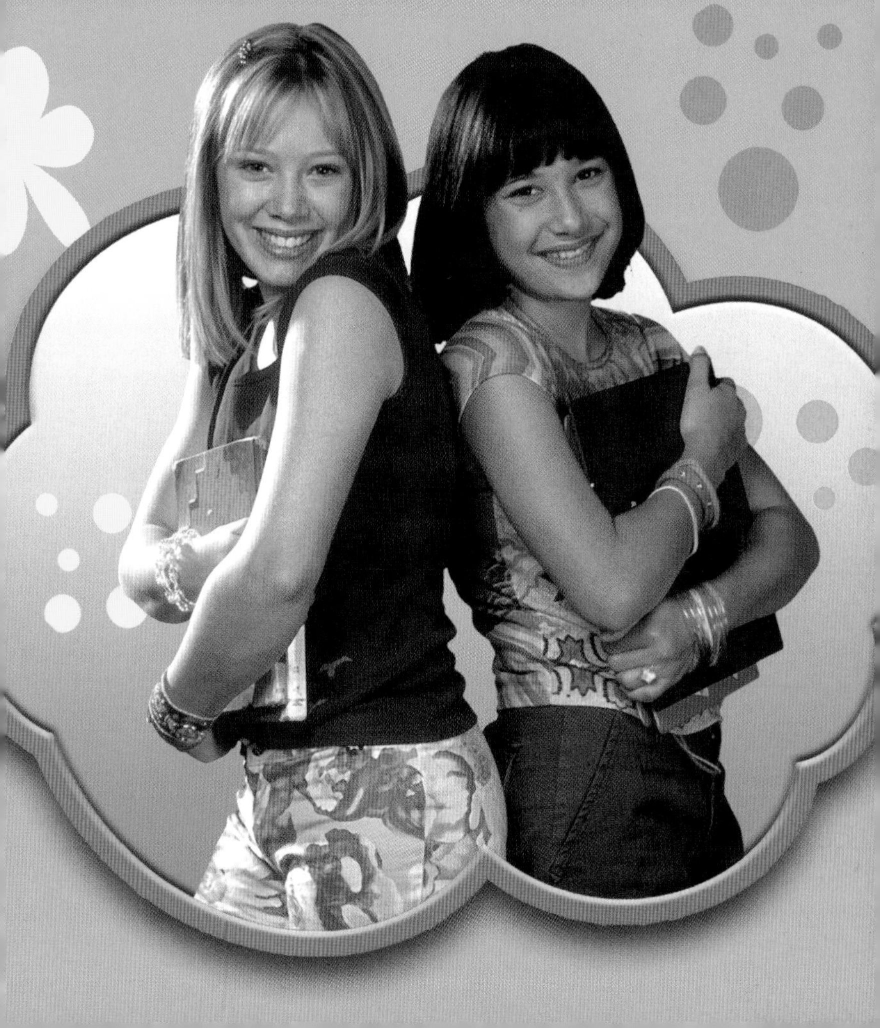

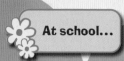

I saw the grossest thing this morning. And it was floating.

In the air?

No, in the water fountain outside the school.

I don't want to hear about this.

I do!

Good morning! Lawrence Tudgeman the third here with your morning announcements. So, whoever put the "you-know-what" in the water fountain this morning, the principal's going to find out who you are Joey, I mean, not that I would tell anybody, Joey...

I would not want to be Joey.

I would not want to be Tudgeman.

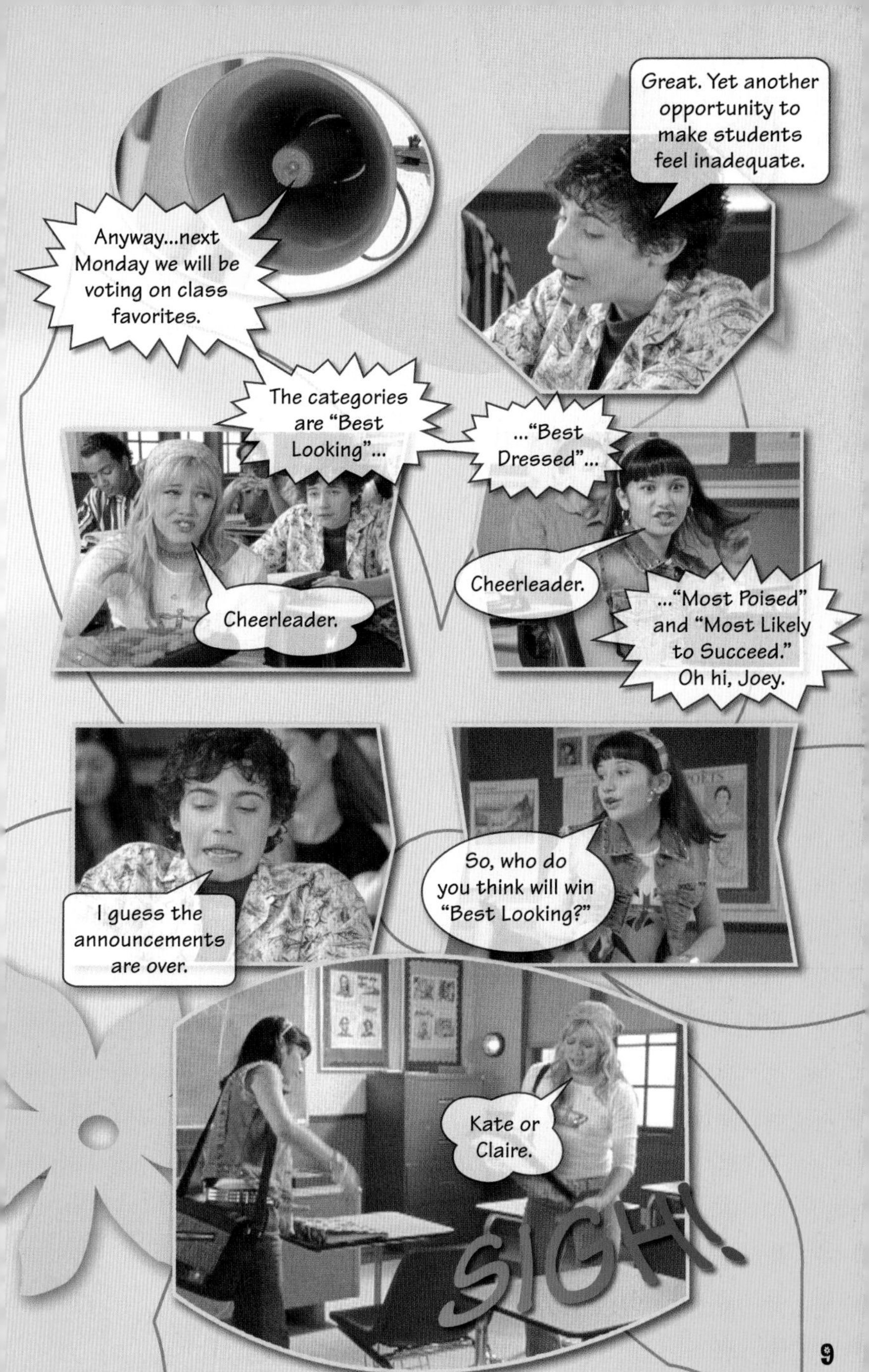

Anyway...next Monday we will be voting on class favorites.
Great. Yet another opportunity to make students feel inadequate.
The categories are "Best Looking"...
..."Best Dressed"...
Cheerleader.
Cheerleader.
..."Most Poised" and "Most Likely to Succeed." Oh hi, Joey.
I guess the announcements are over.
So, who do you think will win "Best Looking?"
Kate or Claire.
SIGH!

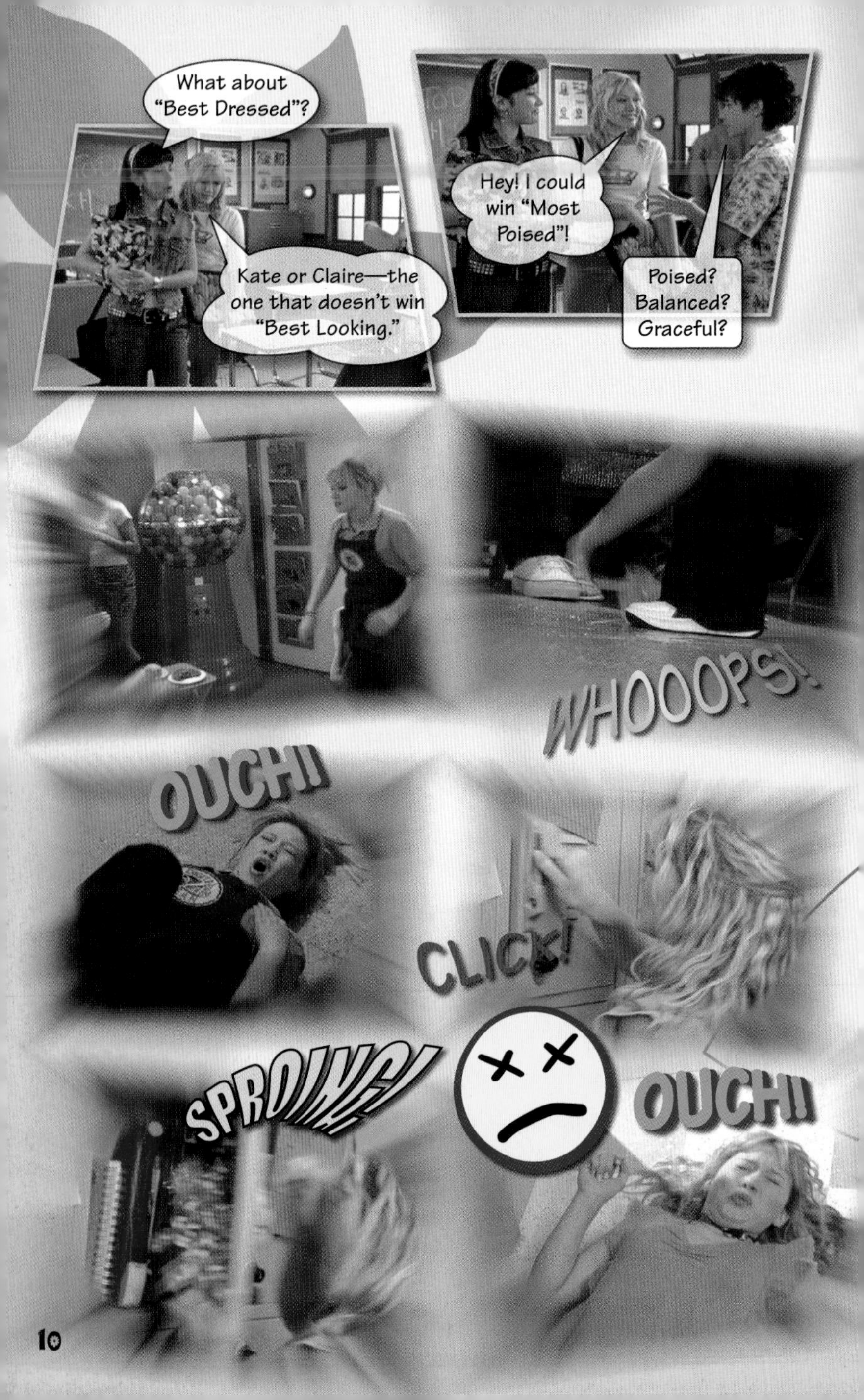
What about "Best Dressed"?
Kate or Claire—the one that doesn't win "Best Looking."
Hey! I could win "Most Poised"!
Poised? Balanced? Graceful?
WHOOOPS!
OUCH!
CLICK!
SPROING!
OUCH!

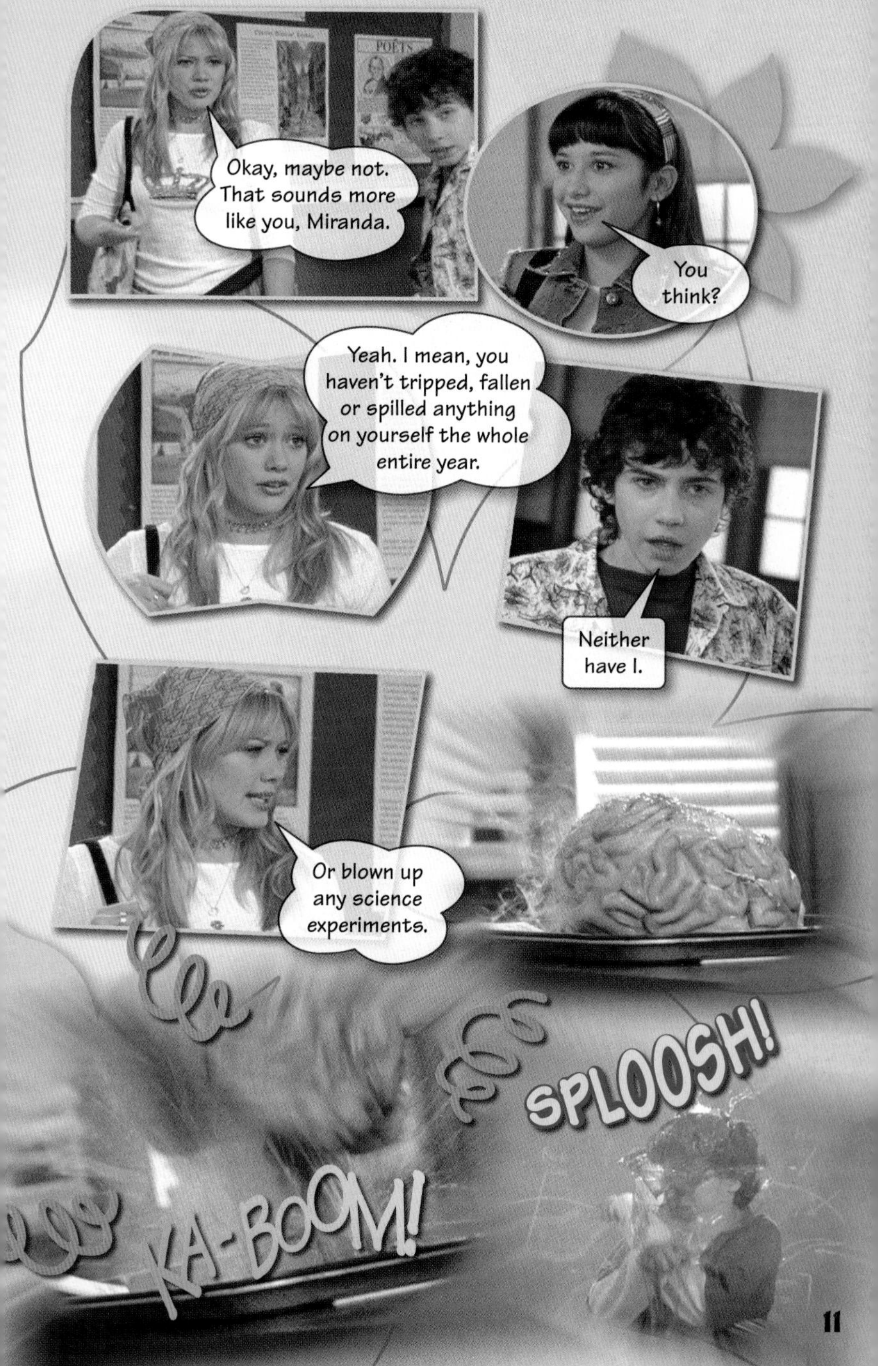
Okay, maybe not. That sounds more like you, Miranda.
You think?
Yeah. I mean, you haven't tripped, fallen or spilled anything on yourself the whole entire year.
Neither have I.
Or blown up any science experiments.
SPLOOSH!
KA-BOOM!

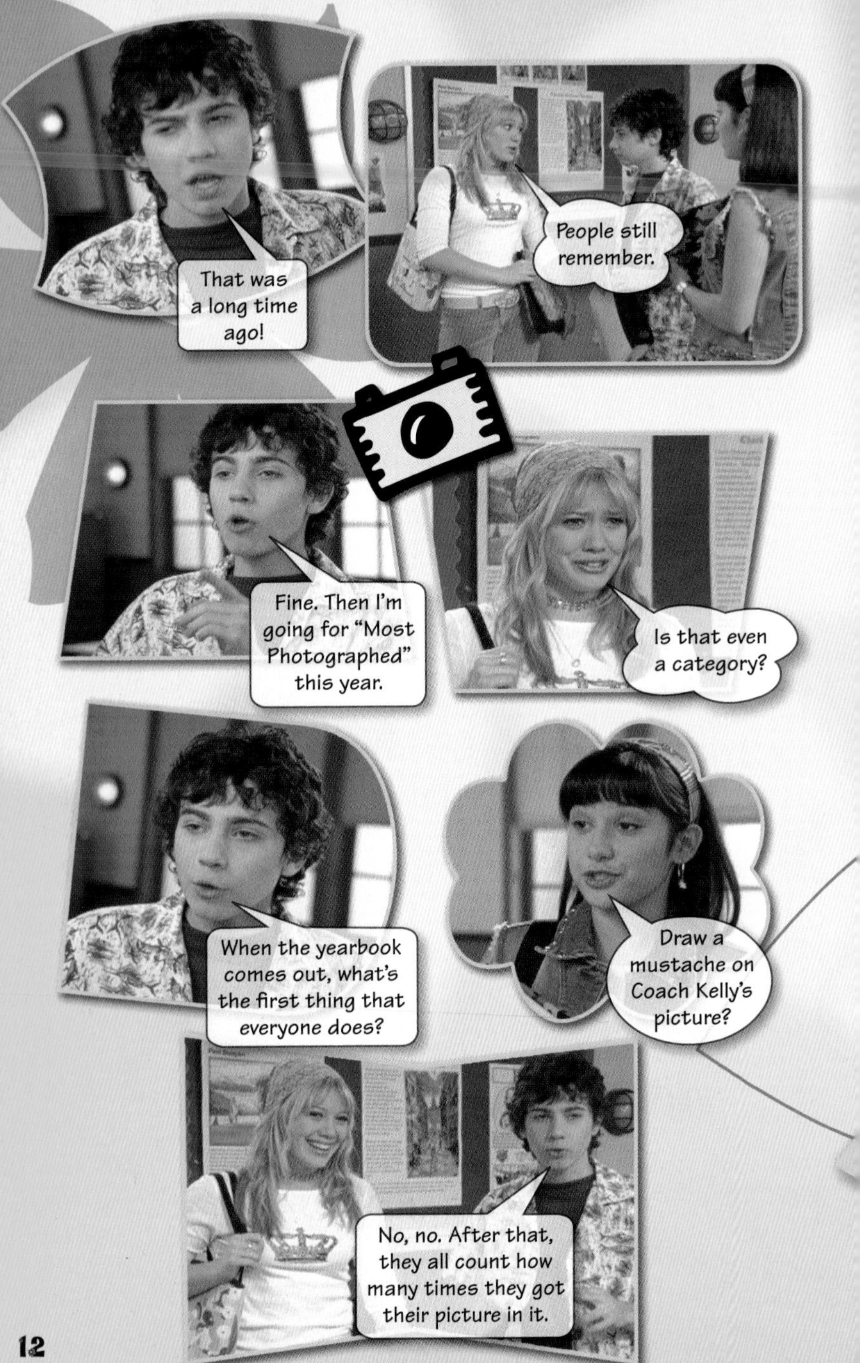
That was a long time ago!
People still remember.
Fine. Then I'm going for "Most Photographed" this year.
Is that even a category?
When the yearbook comes out, what's the first thing that everyone does?
Draw a mustache on Coach Kelly's picture?
No, no. After that, they all count how many times they got their picture in it.

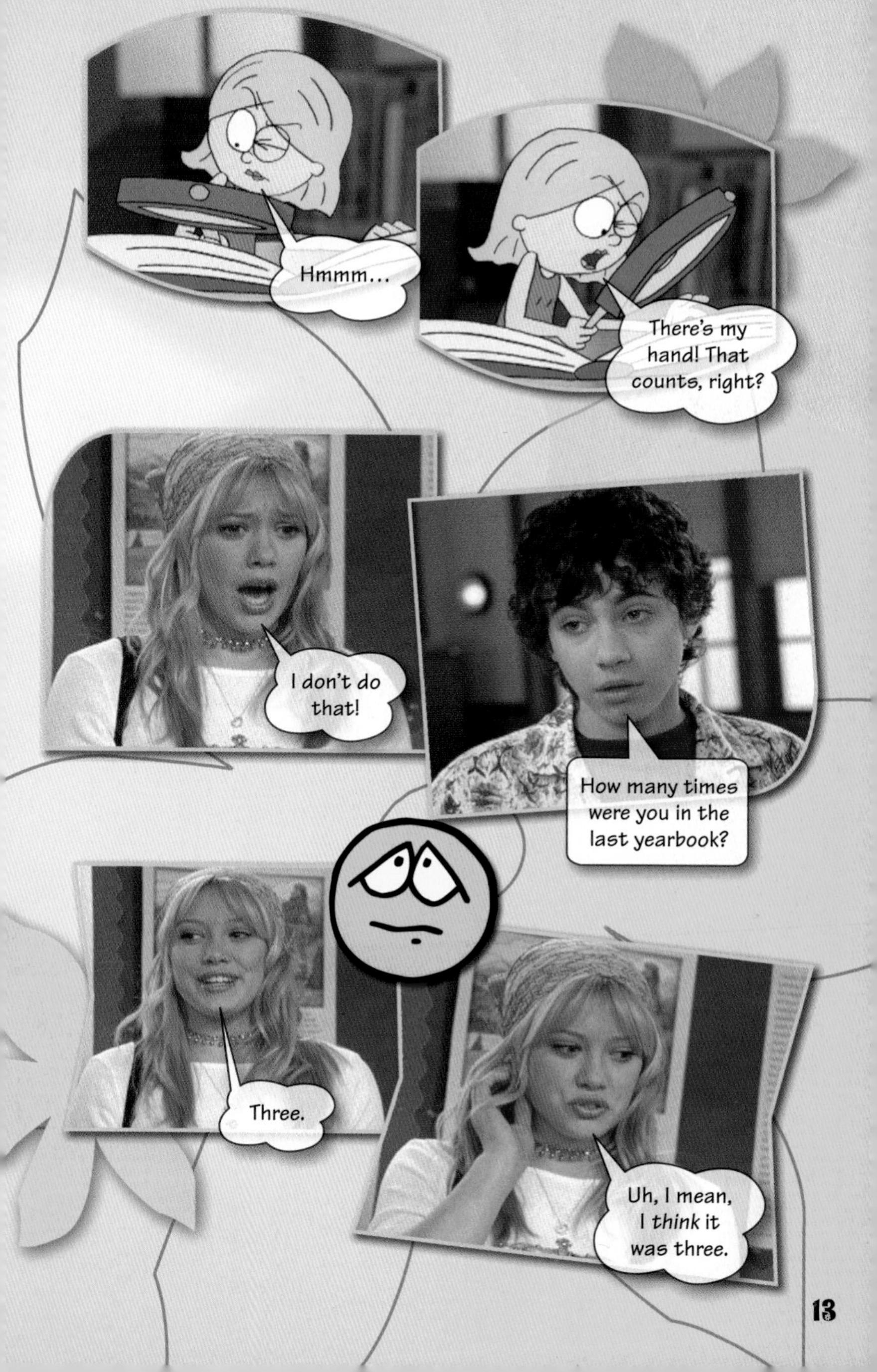
Hmmm...
There's my hand! That counts, right?
I don't do that!
How many times were you in the last yearbook?
Three.
Uh, I mean, I *think* it was three.

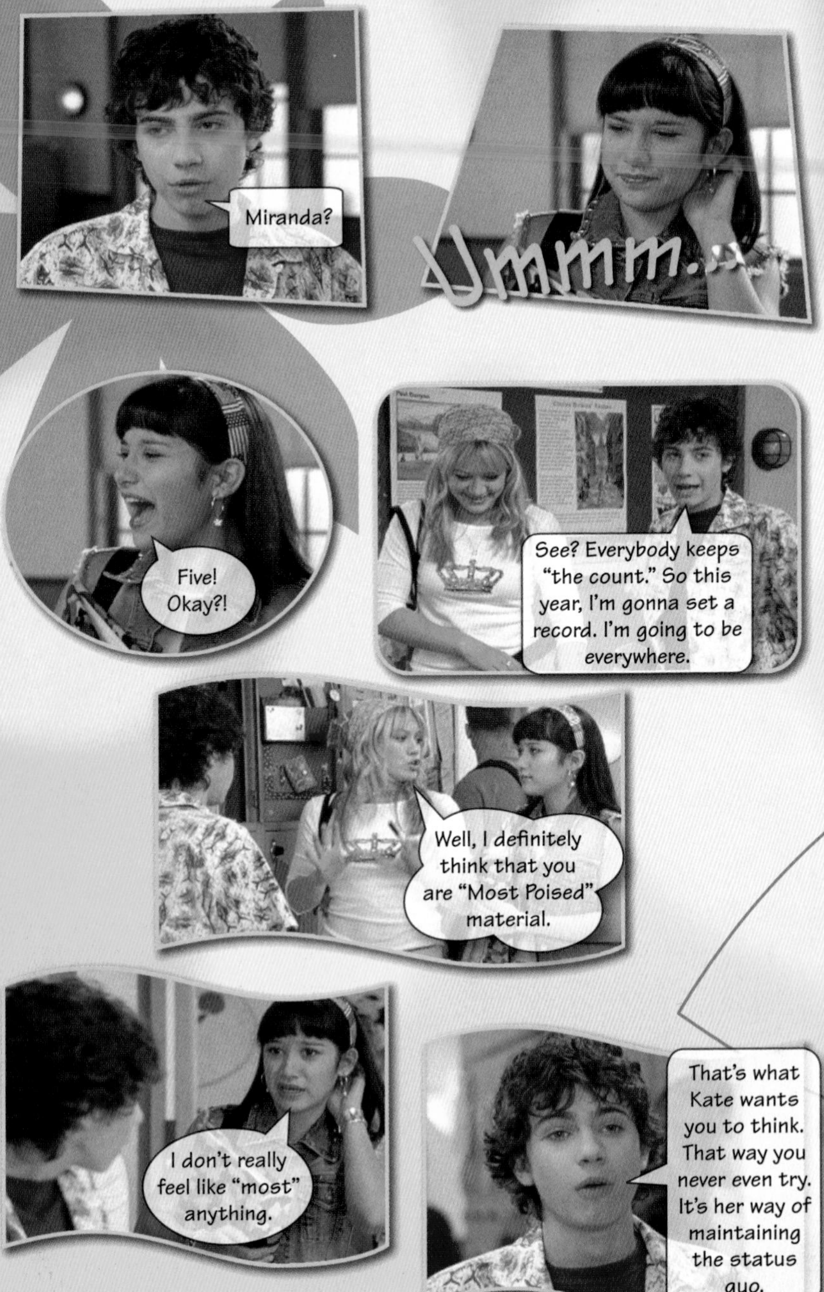
Miranda?
Ummm...
Five! Okay?!
See? Everybody keeps "the count." So this year, I'm gonna set a record. I'm going to be everywhere.
Well, I definitely think that you are "Most Poised" material.
I don't really feel like "most" anything.
That's what Kate wants you to think. That way you never even try. It's her way of maintaining the status quo.

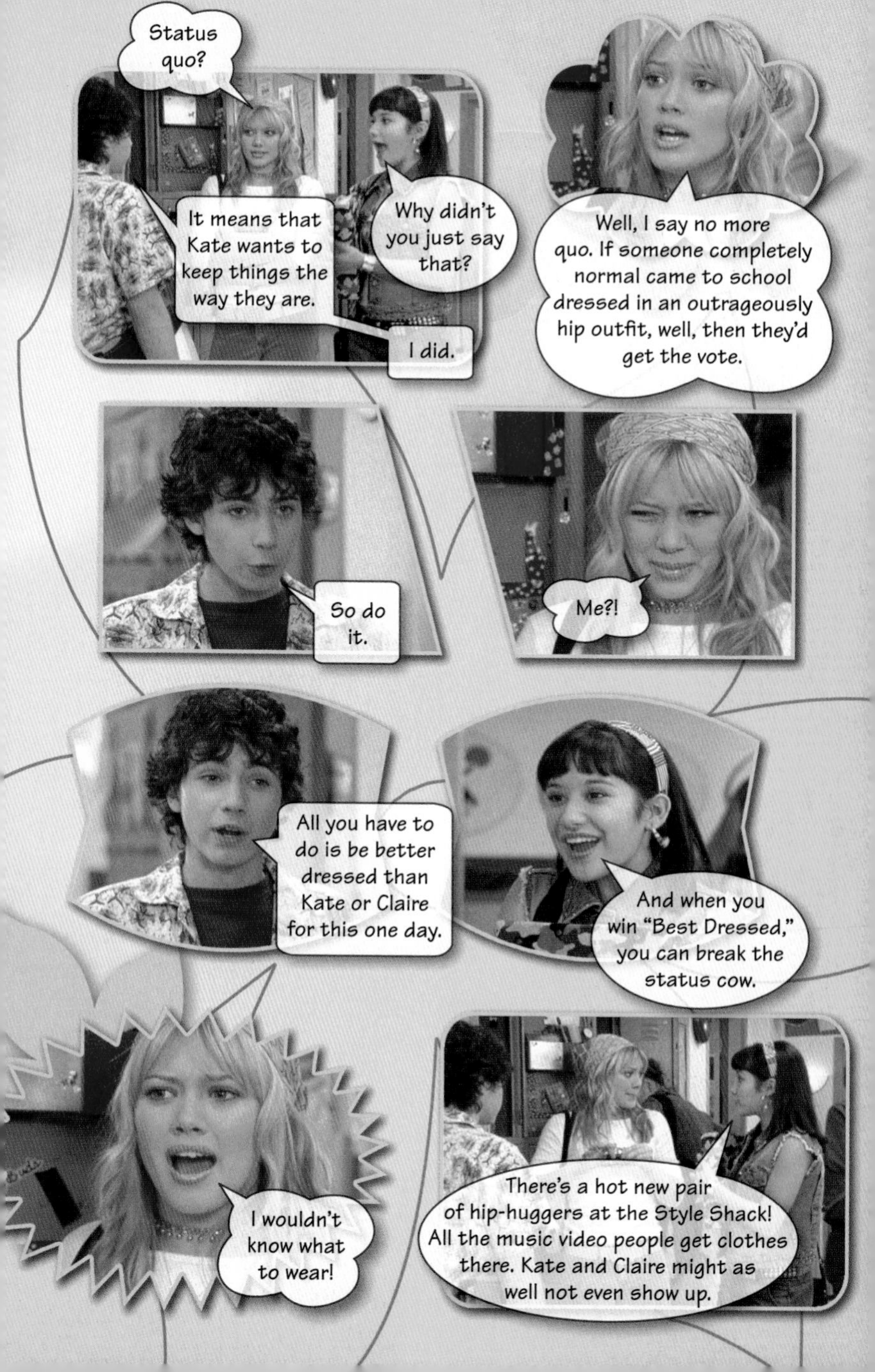

Status quo?
It means that Kate wants to keep things the way they are.
Why didn't you just say that?
I did.
Well, I say no more quo. If someone completely normal came to school dressed in an outrageously hip outfit, well, then they'd get the vote.
So do it.
Me?!
All you have to do is be better dressed than Kate or Claire for this one day.
And when you win "Best Dressed," you can break the status cow.
I wouldn't know what to wear!
There's a hot new pair of hip-huggers at the Style Shack! All the music video people get clothes there. Kate and Claire might as well not even show up.

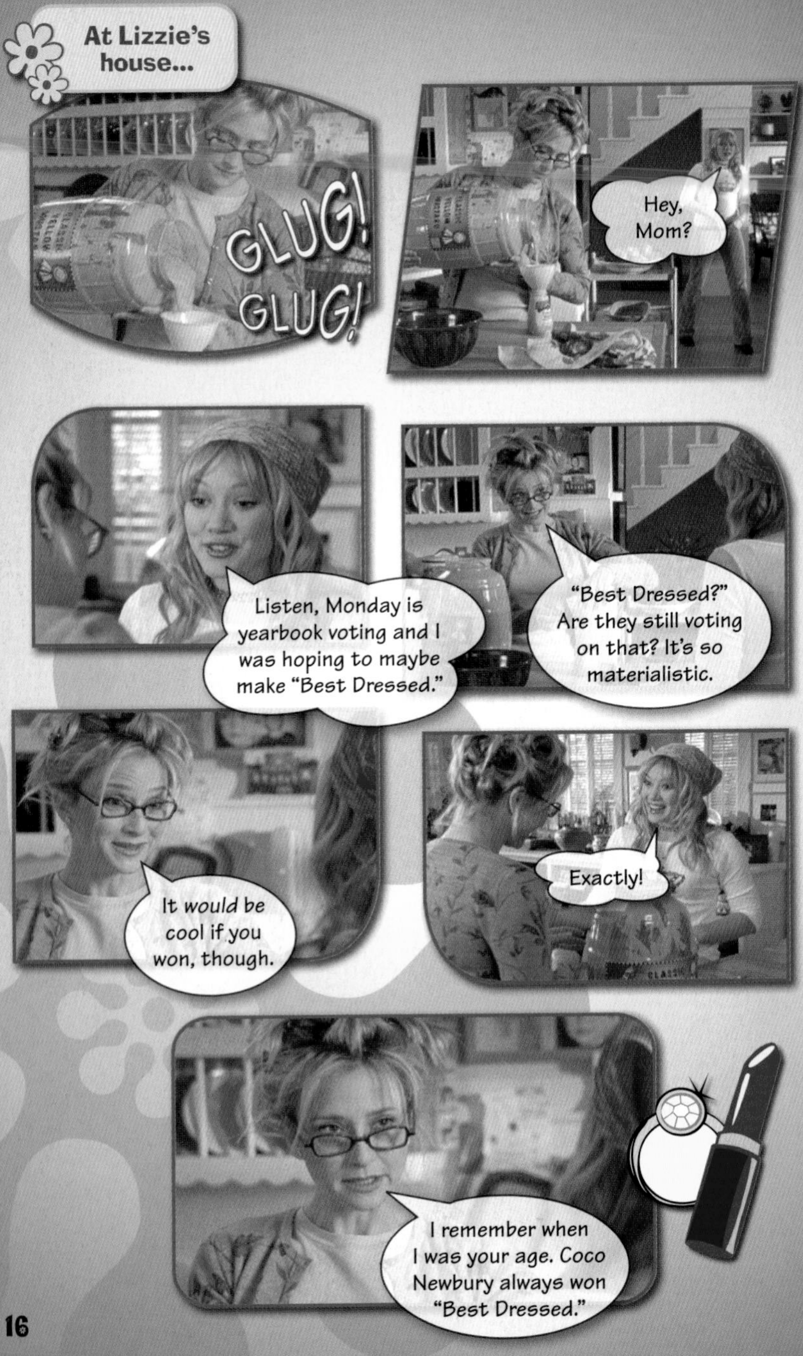
At Lizzie's house...
GLUG! GLUG!
Hey, Mom?
Listen, Monday is yearbook voting and I was hoping to maybe make "Best Dressed."
"Best Dressed?" Are they still voting on that? It's so materialistic.
It would be cool if you won, though.
Exactly!
I remember when I was your age. Coco Newbury always won "Best Dressed."

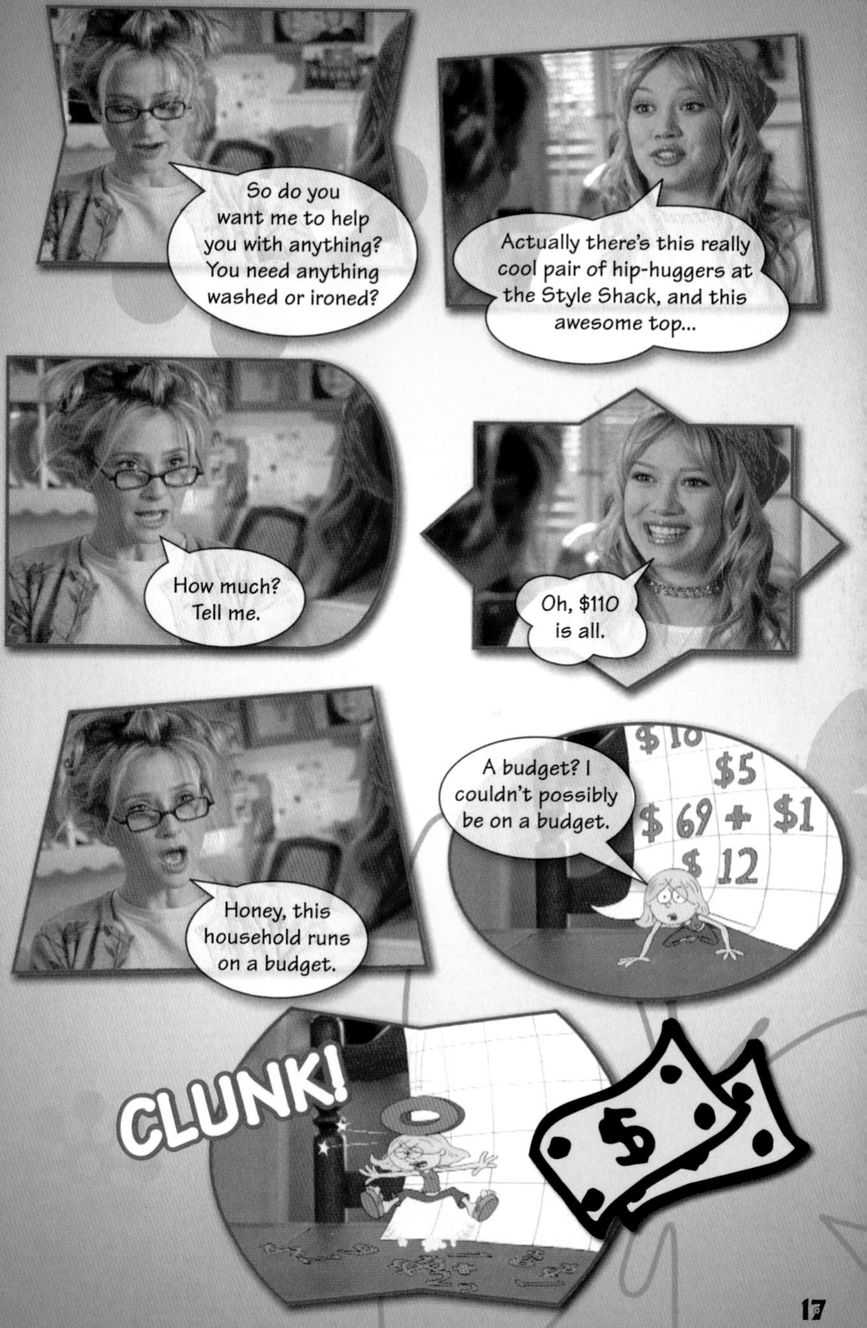
So do you want me to help you with anything? You need anything washed or ironed?
Actually there's this really cool pair of hip-huggers at the Style Shack, and this awesome top...
How much? Tell me.
Oh, $110 is all.
Honey, this household runs on a budget.
A budget? I couldn't possibly be on a budget.
$5
$ 69 + $1
$ 12
CLUNK!

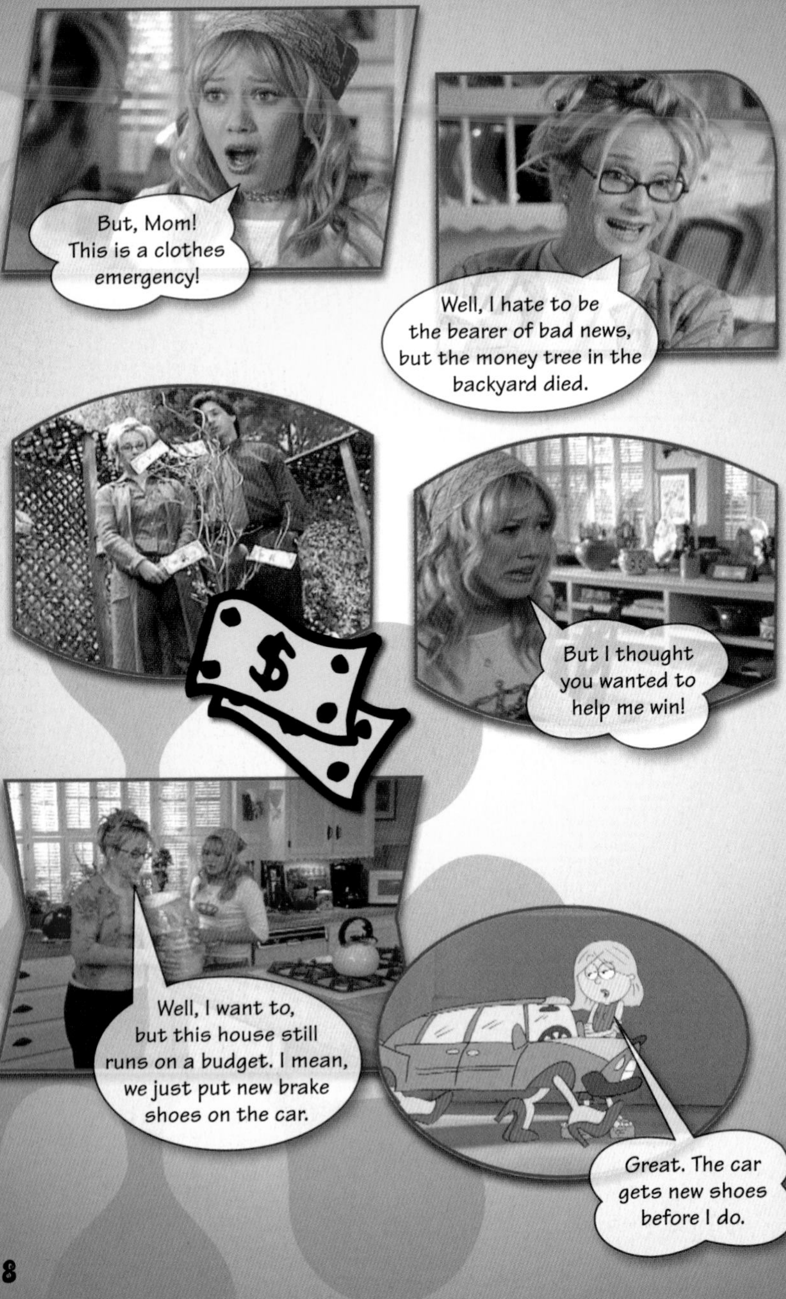
But, Mom! This is a clothes emergency!
Well, I hate to be the bearer of bad news, but the money tree in the backyard died.
But I thought you wanted to help me win!
Well, I want to, but this house still runs on a budget. I mean, we just put new brake shoes on the car.
Great. The car gets new shoes before I do.

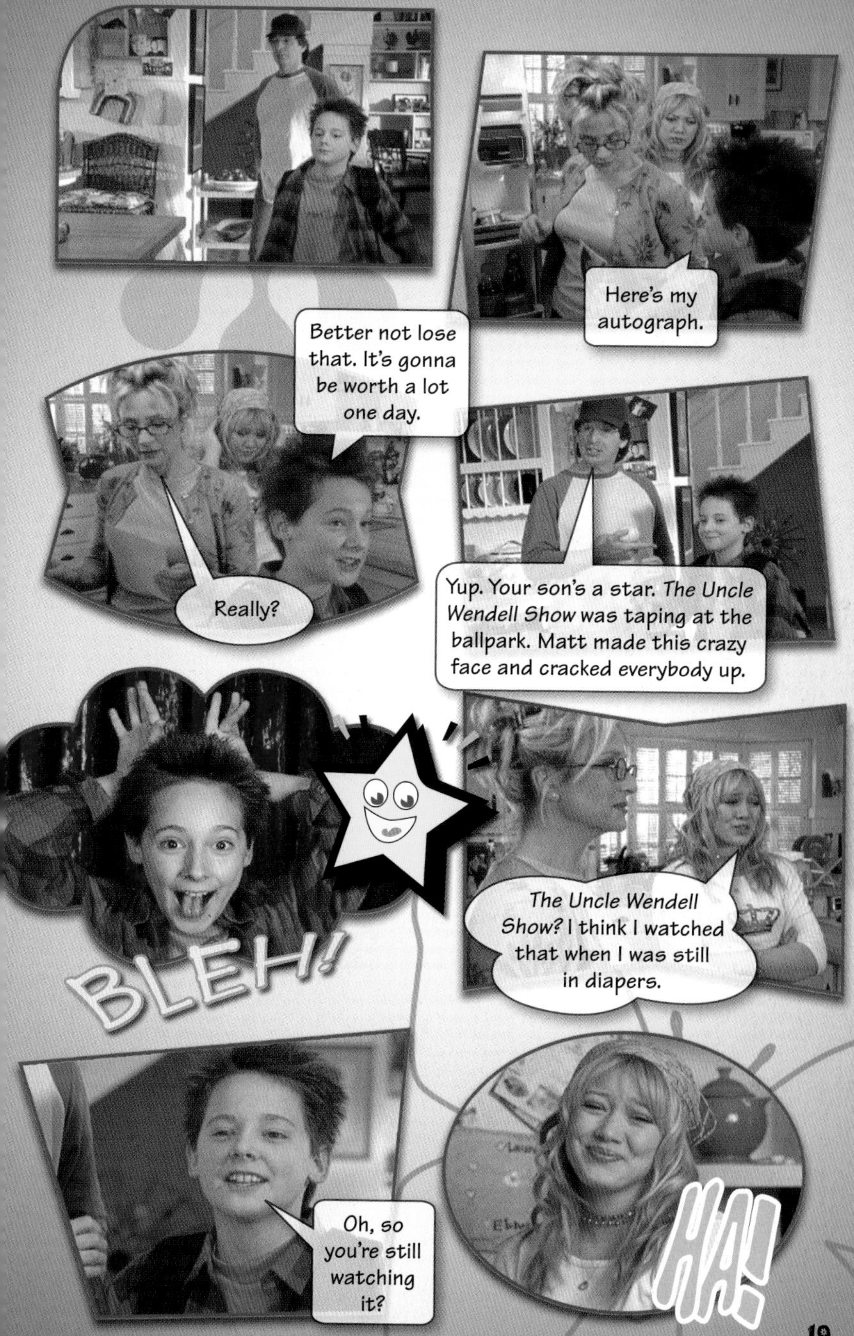

Here's my autograph.
Better not lose that. It's gonna be worth a lot one day.
Really?
Yup. Your son's a star. *The Uncle Wendell Show* was taping at the ballpark. Matt made this crazy face and cracked everybody up.
BLEH!
The Uncle Wendell Show? I think I watched that when I was still in diapers.
Oh, so you're still watching it?
HA!

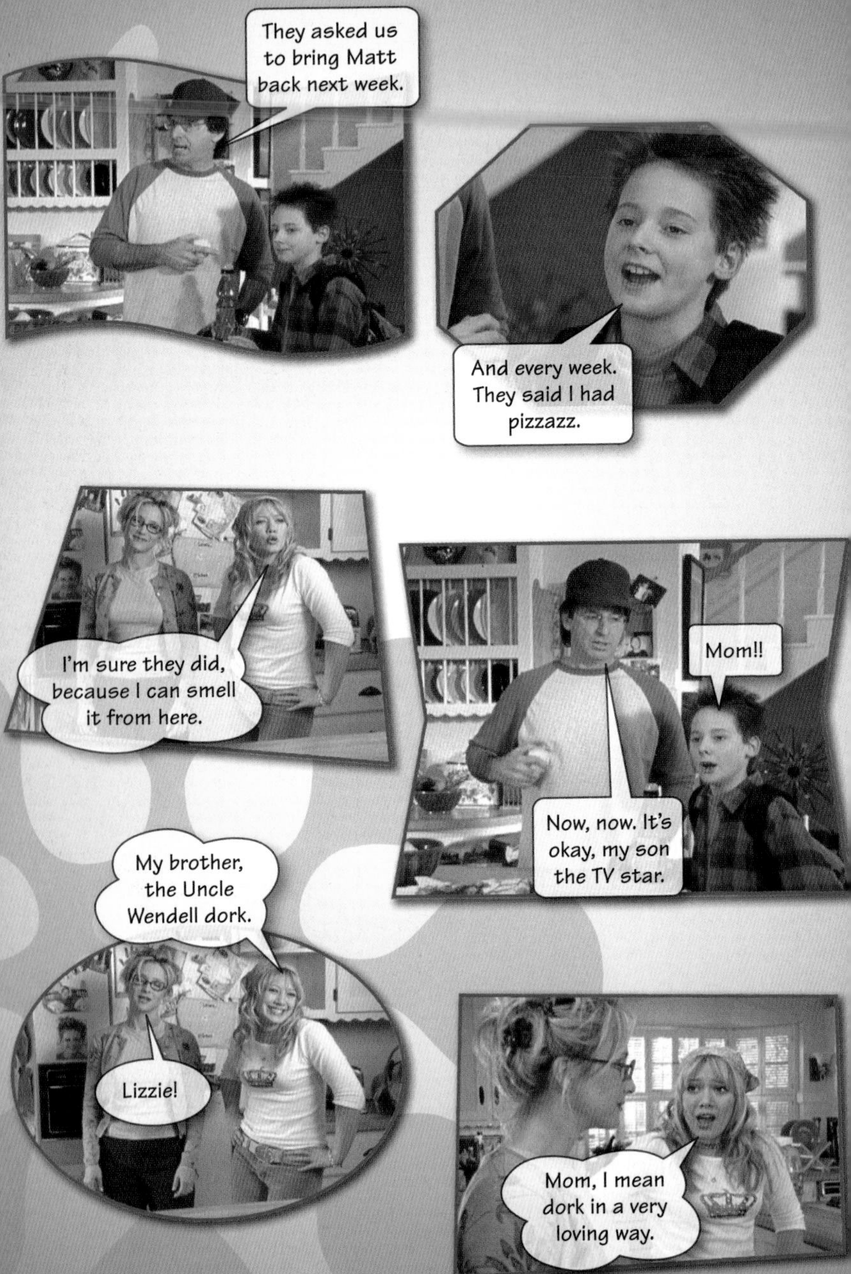
They asked us to bring Matt back next week.
And every week. They said I had pizzazz.
I'm sure they did, because I can smell it from here.
Mom!!
Now, now. It's okay, my son the TV star.
My brother, the Uncle Wendell dork.
Lizzie!
Mom, I mean dork in a very loving way.

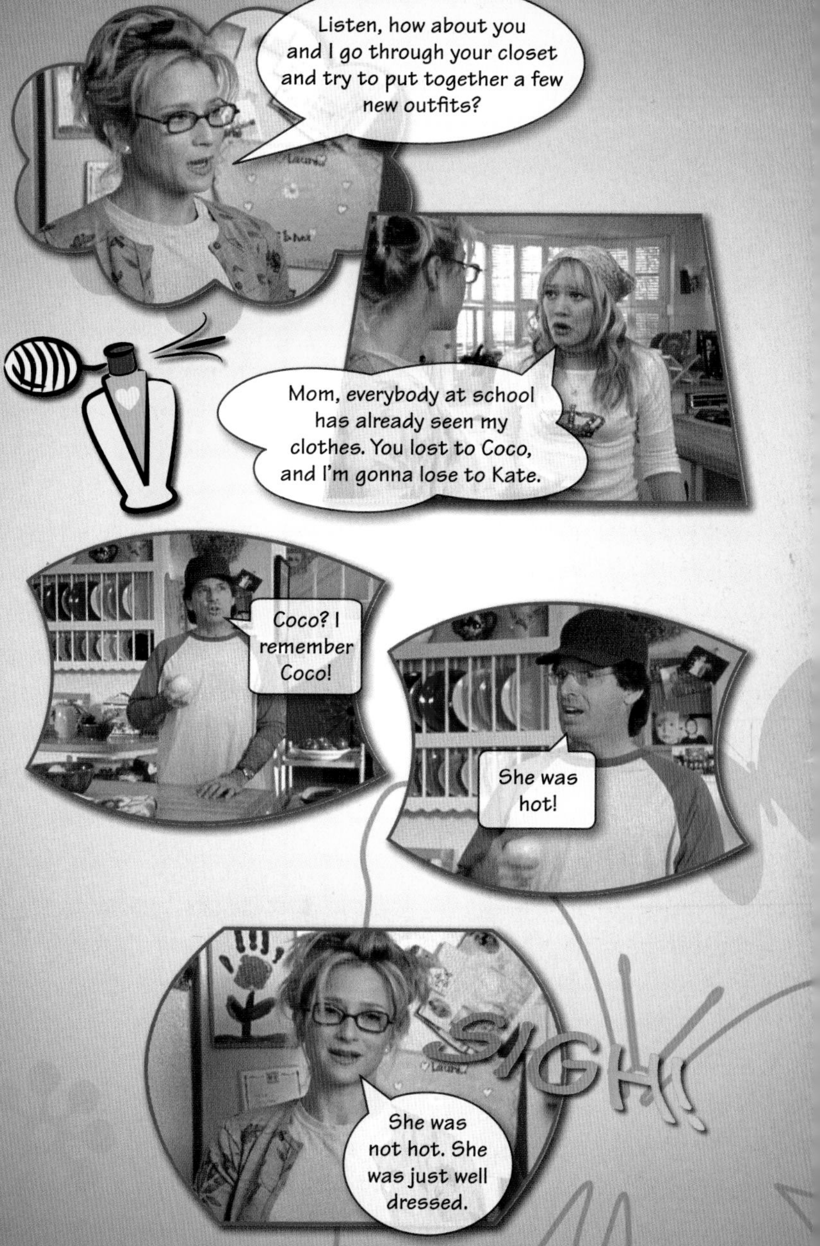
Listen, how about you and I go through your closet and try to put together a few new outfits?
Mom, everybody at school has already seen my clothes. You lost to Coco, and I'm gonna lose to Kate.
Coco? I remember Coco!
She was hot!
She was not hot. She was just well dressed.
SIGH!!

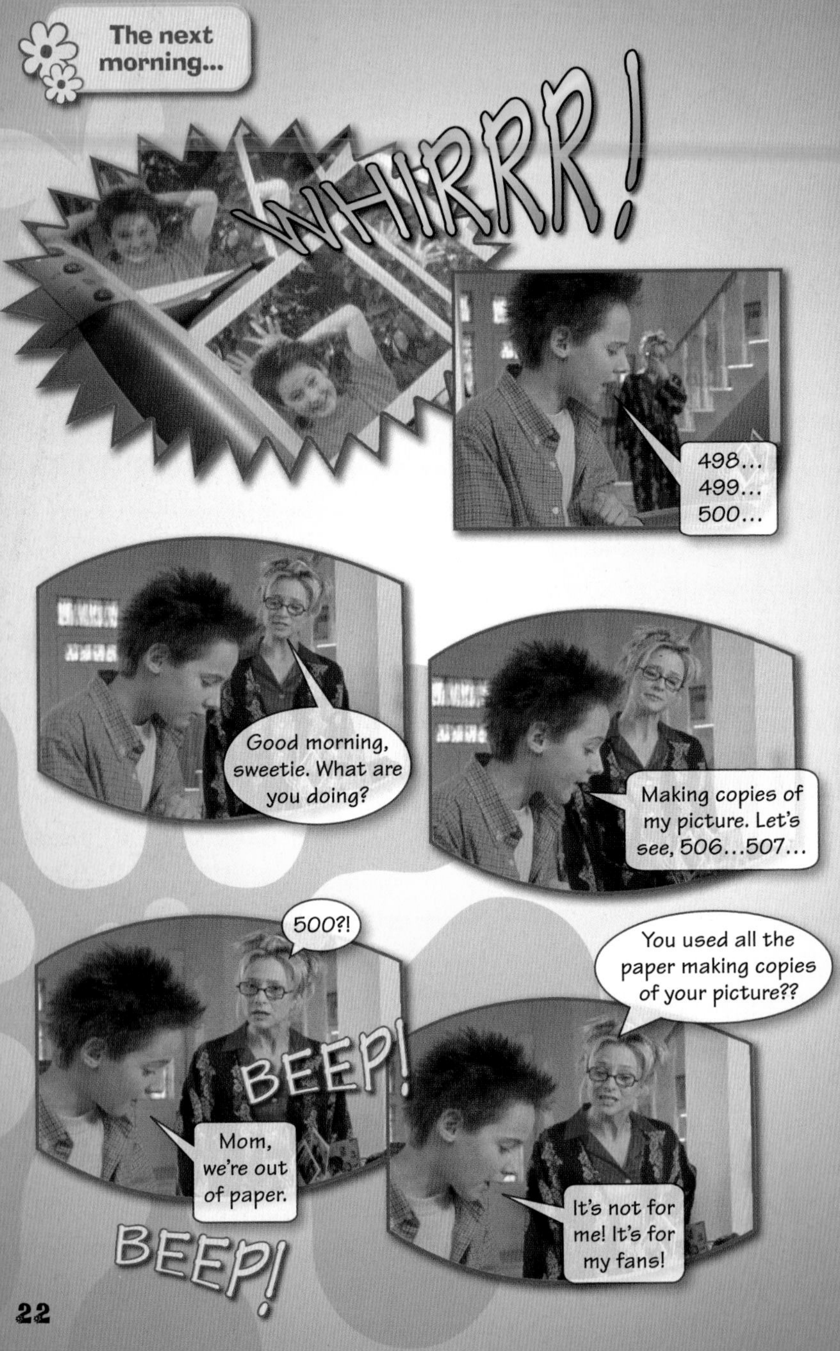
The next morning...
WHIRRR!
498...
499...
500...
Good morning, sweetie. What are you doing?
Making copies of my picture. Let's see, 506...507...
500?!
Mom, we're out of paper.
BEEP!
BEEP!
You used all the paper making copies of your picture??
It's not for me! It's for my fans!

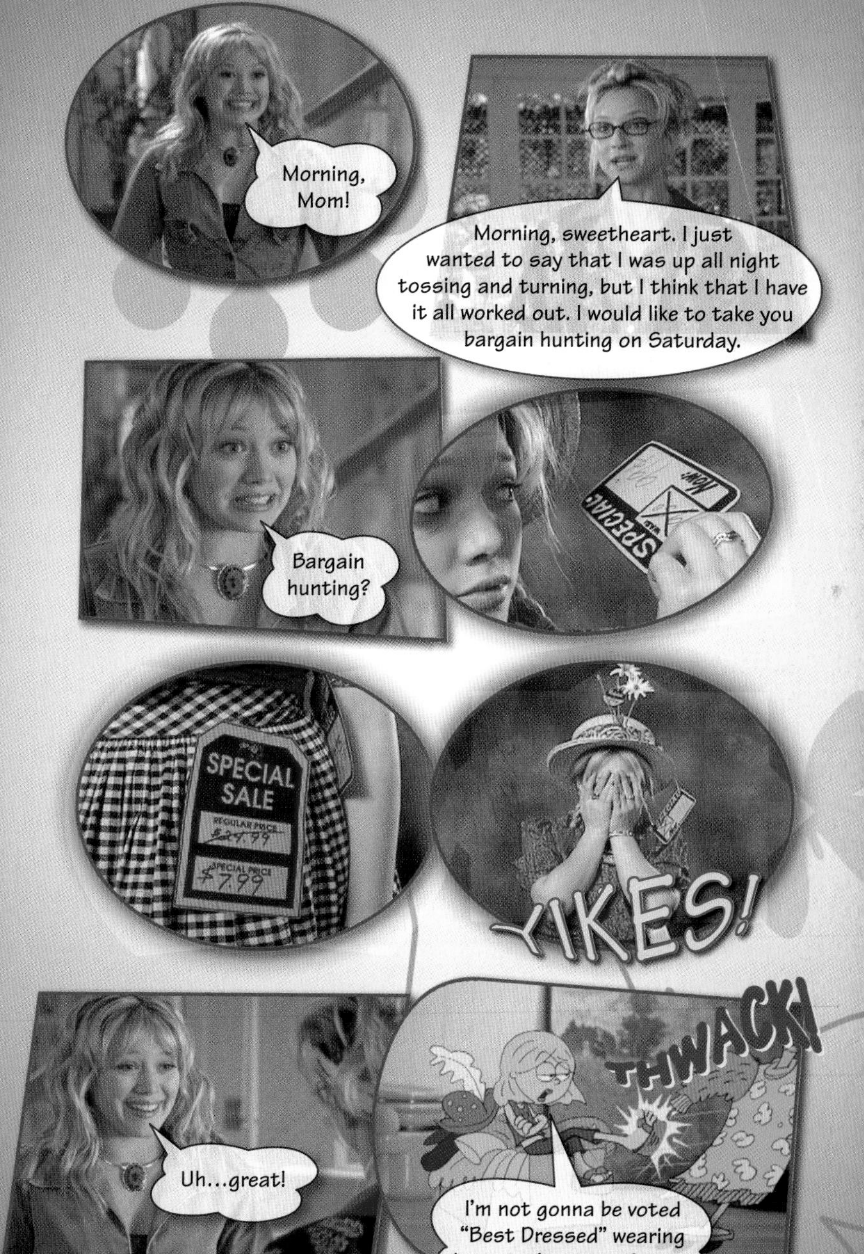
Morning, Mom!
Morning, sweetheart. I just wanted to say that I was up all night tossing and turning, but I think that I have it all worked out. I would like to take you bargain hunting on Saturday.
Bargain hunting?
SPECIAL SALE
REGULAR PRICE
$24.99
SPECIAL PRICE
$7.99
YIKES!
Uh...great!
THWACK!
I'm not gonna be voted "Best Dressed" wearing last year's rejects from a bargain store.

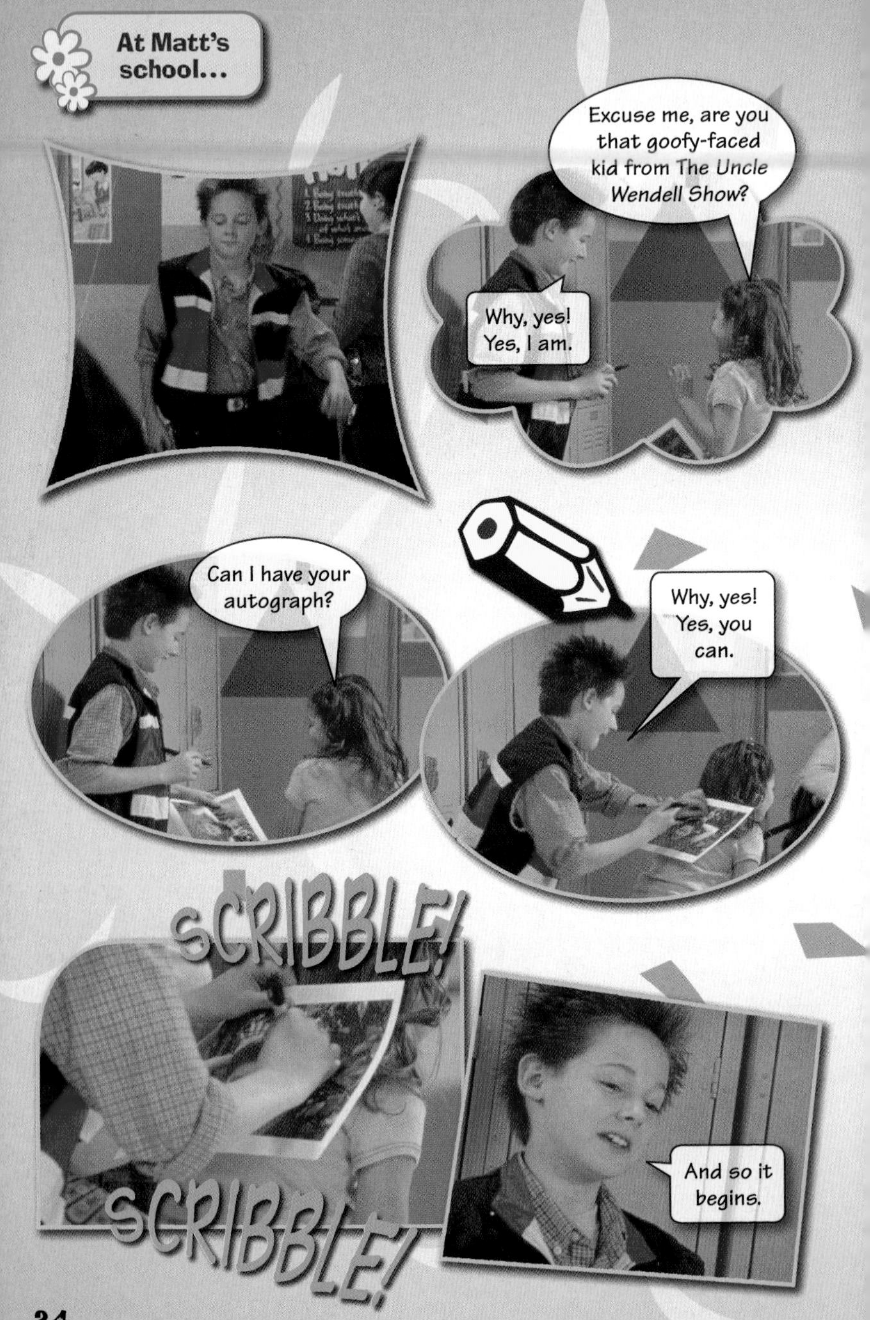

At Matt's school...
Excuse me, are you that goofy-faced kid from The Uncle Wendell Show?
Why, yes! Yes, I am.
Can I have your autograph?
Why, yes! Yes, you can.
SCRIBBLE!
SCRIBBLE!
And so it begins.

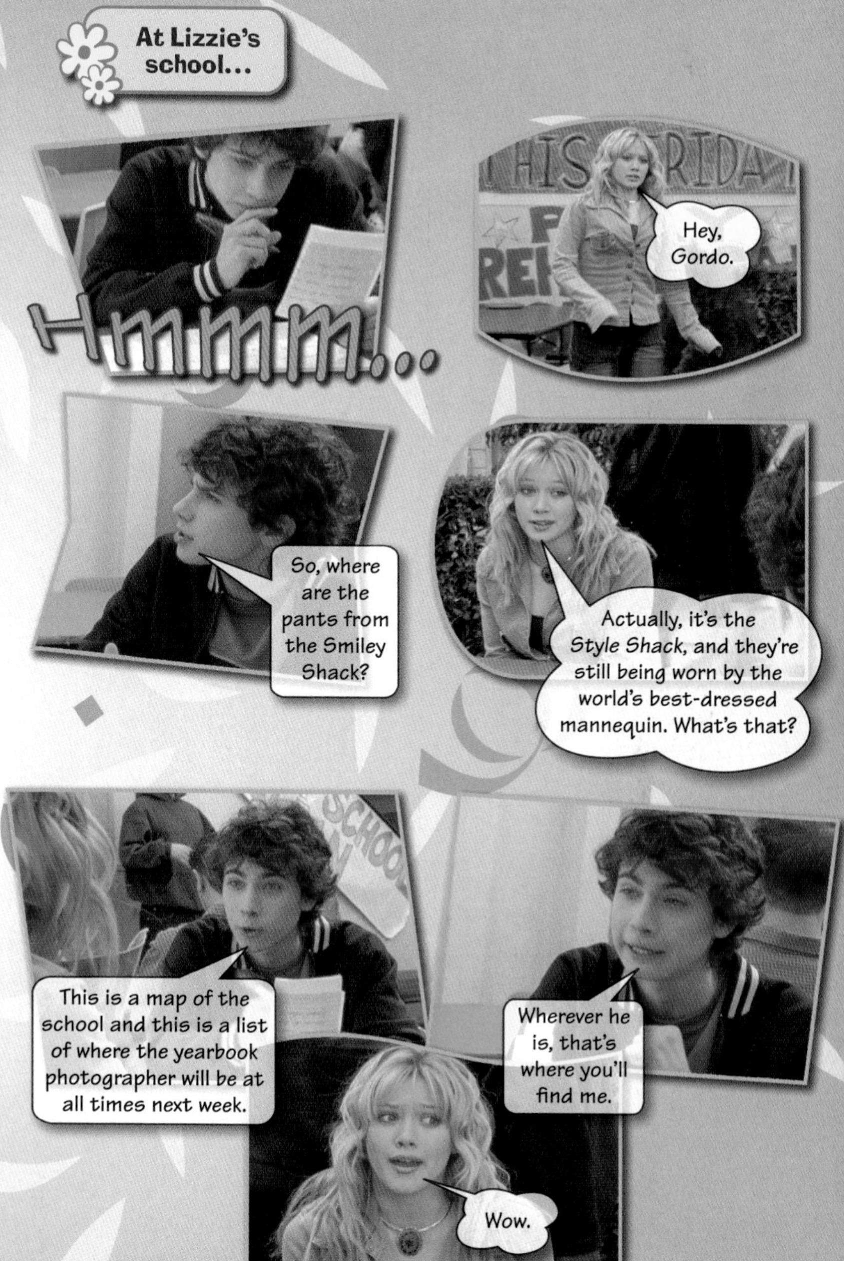
At Lizzie's school...
Hmmmm...
Hey, Gordo.
So, where are the pants from the Smiley Shack?
Actually, it's the *Style Shack*, and they're still being worn by the world's best-dressed mannequin. What's that?
This is a map of the school and this is a list of where the yearbook photographer will be at all times next week.
Wherever he is, that's where you'll find me.
Wow.

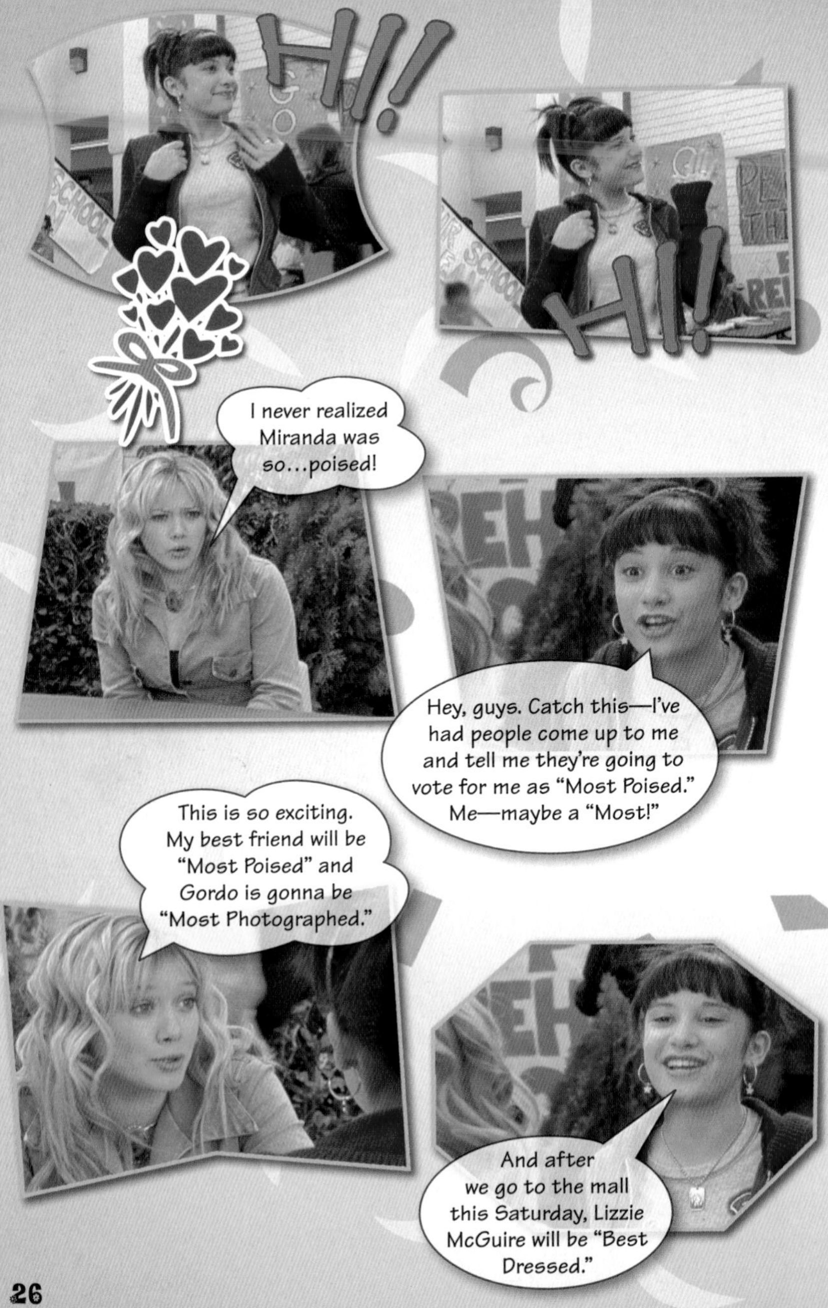

HI!
HI!
I never realized Miranda was so...poised!
Hey, guys. Catch this—I've had people come up to me and tell me they're going to vote for me as "Most Poised." Me—maybe a "Most!"
This is so exciting. My best friend will be "Most Poised" and Gordo is gonna be "Most Photographed."
And after we go to the mall this Saturday, Lizzie McGuire will be "Best Dressed."

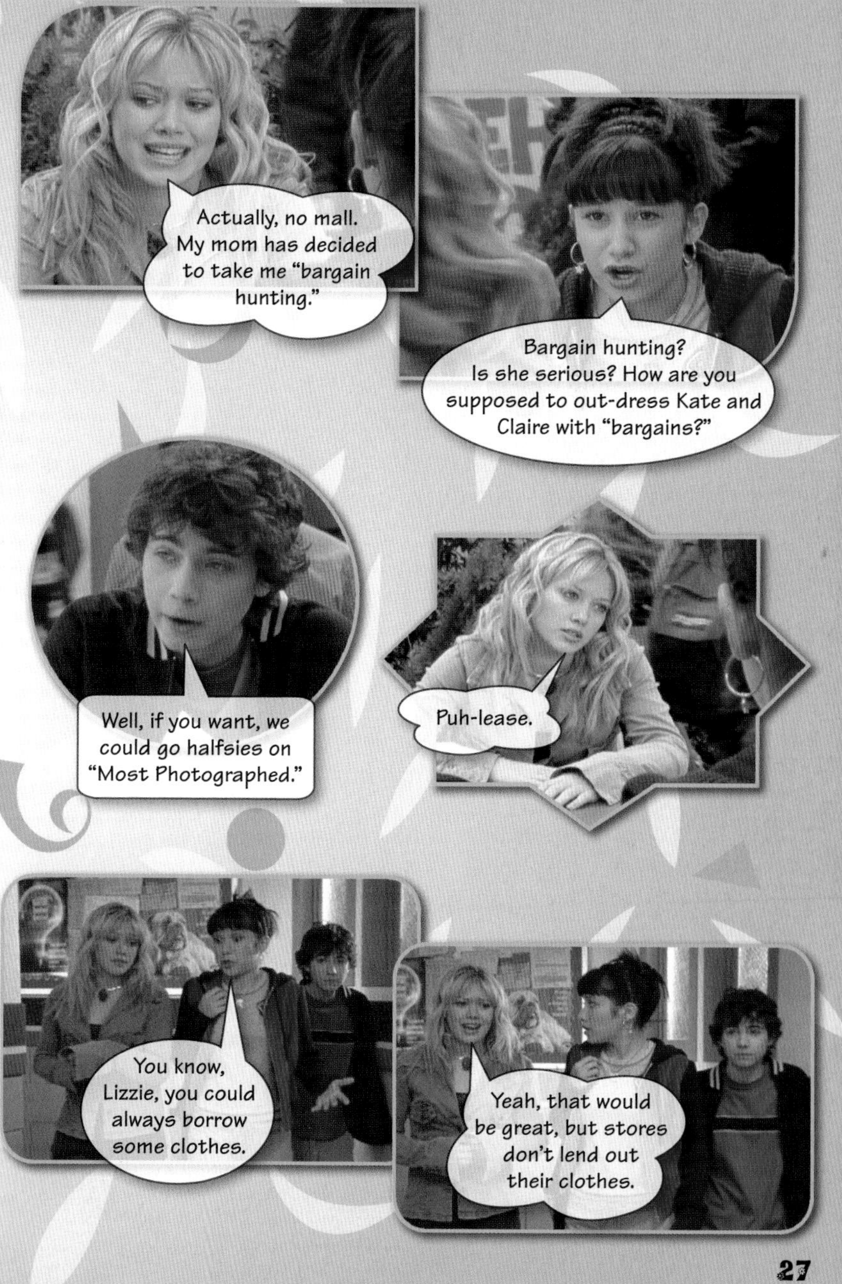
Actually, no mall. My mom has decided to take me "bargain hunting."
Bargain hunting? Is she serious? How are you supposed to out-dress Kate and Claire with "bargains?"
Well, if you want, we could go halfsies on "Most Photographed."
Puh-lease.
You know, Lizzie, you could always borrow some clothes.
Yeah, that would be great, but stores don't lend out their clothes.

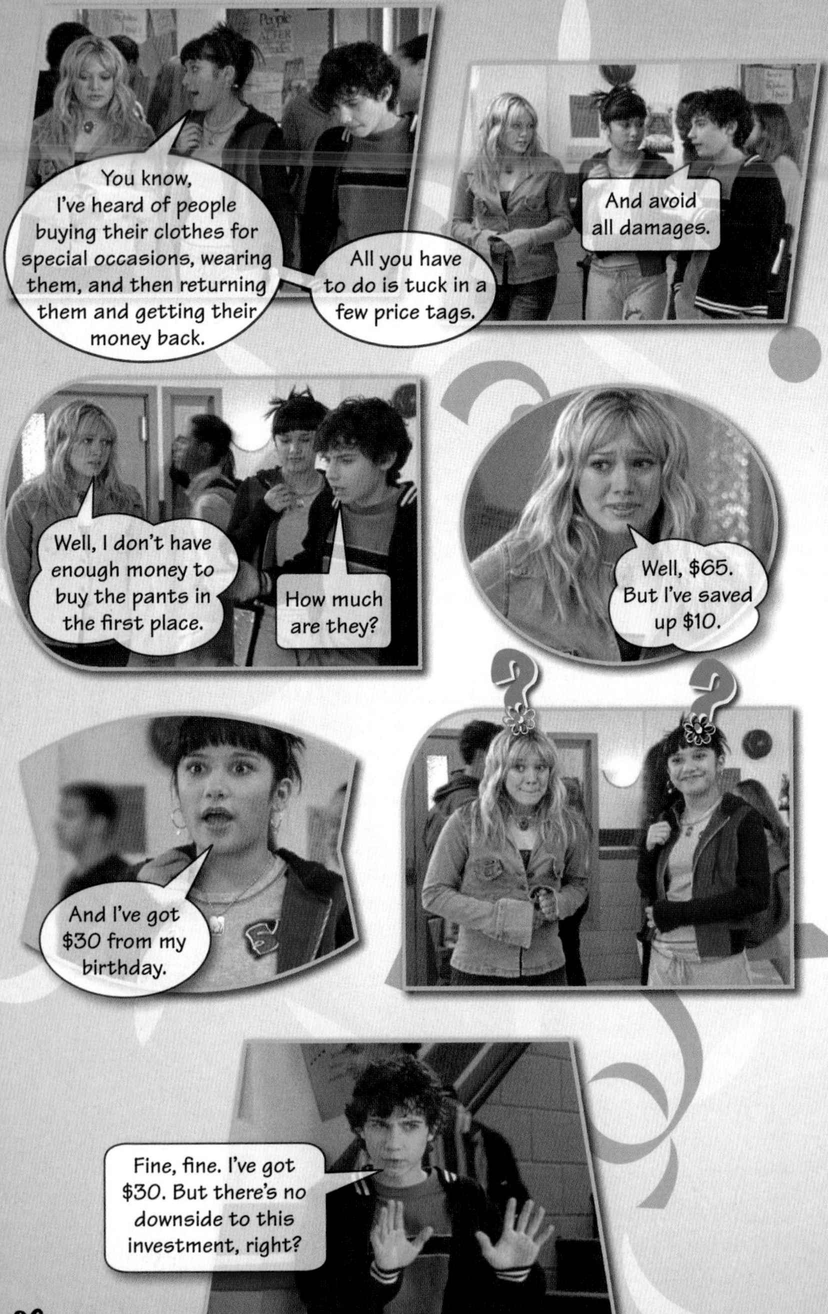
You know, I've heard of people buying their clothes for special occasions, wearing them, and then returning them and getting their money back.
All you have to do is tuck in a few price tags.
And avoid all damages.
Well, I don't have enough money to buy the pants in the first place.
How much are they?
Well, $65. But I've saved up $10.
And I've got $30 from my birthday.
Fine, fine. I've got $30. But there's no downside to this investment, right?

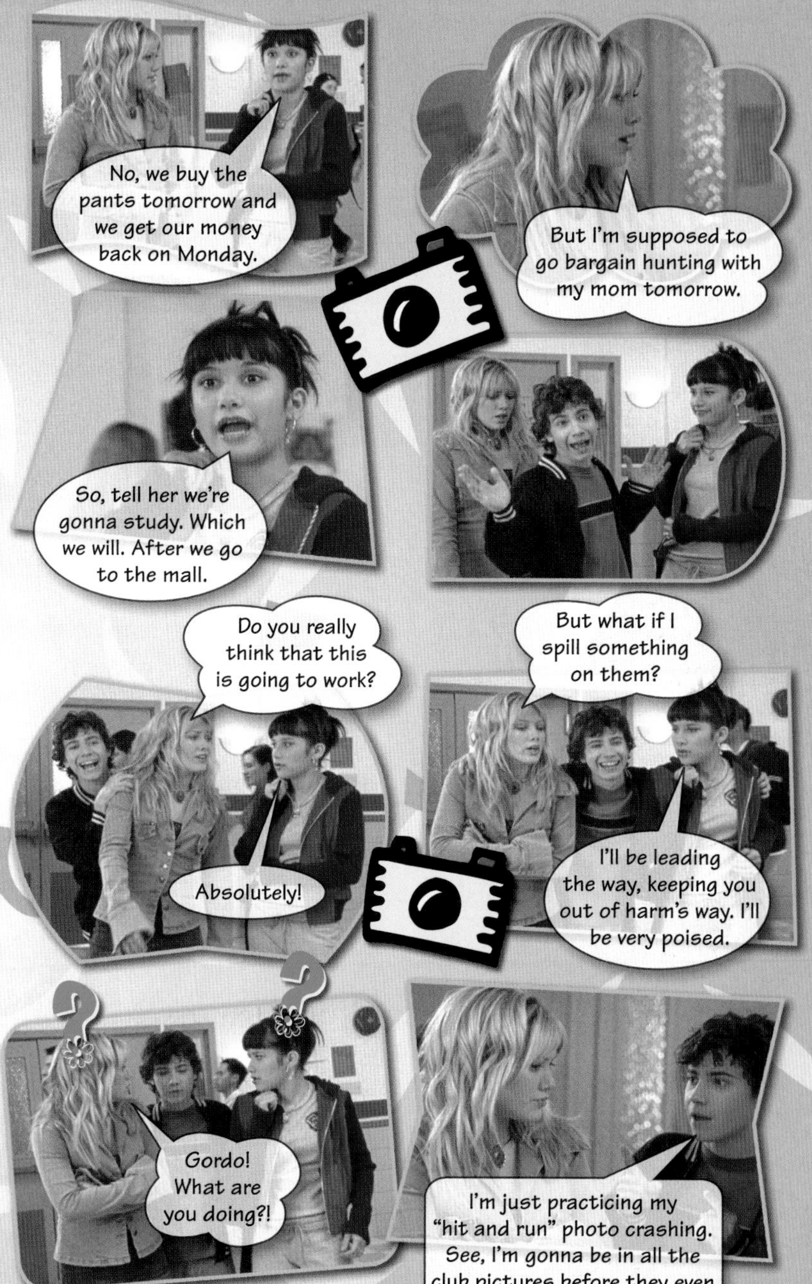
No, we buy the pants tomorrow and we get our money back on Monday.
But I'm supposed to go bargain hunting with my mom tomorrow.
So, tell her we're gonna study. Which we will. After we go to the mall.
Do you really think that this is going to work?
Absolutely!
But what if I spill something on them?
I'll be leading the way, keeping you out of harm's way. I'll be very poised.
Gordo! What are you doing?!
I'm just practicing my "hit and run" photo crashing. See, I'm gonna be in all the club pictures before they even realize I'm not in their club.

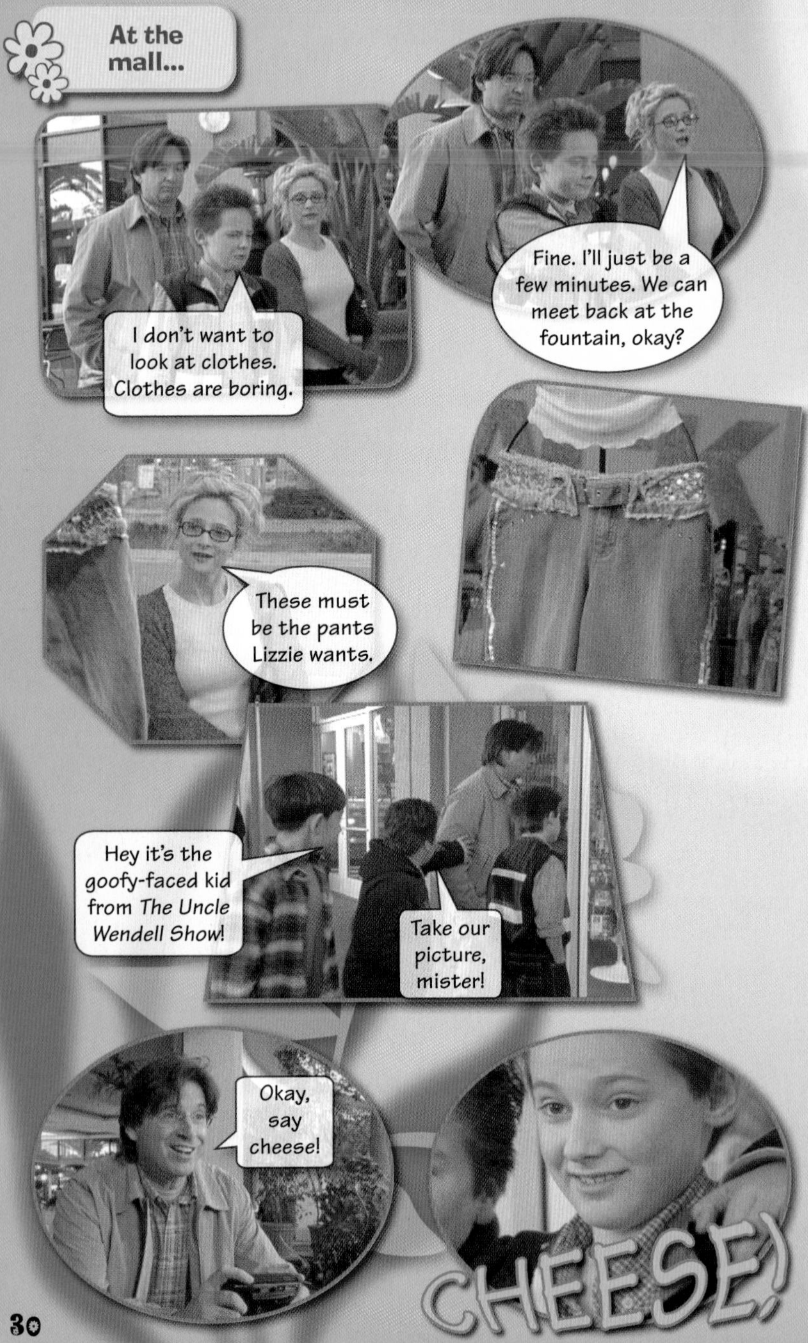
At the mall...
I don't want to look at clothes. Clothes are boring.
Fine. I'll just be a few minutes. We can meet back at the fountain, okay?
These must be the pants Lizzie wants.
Hey it's the goofy-faced kid from The Uncle Wendell Show!
Take our picture, mister!
Okay, say cheese!
CHEESE!

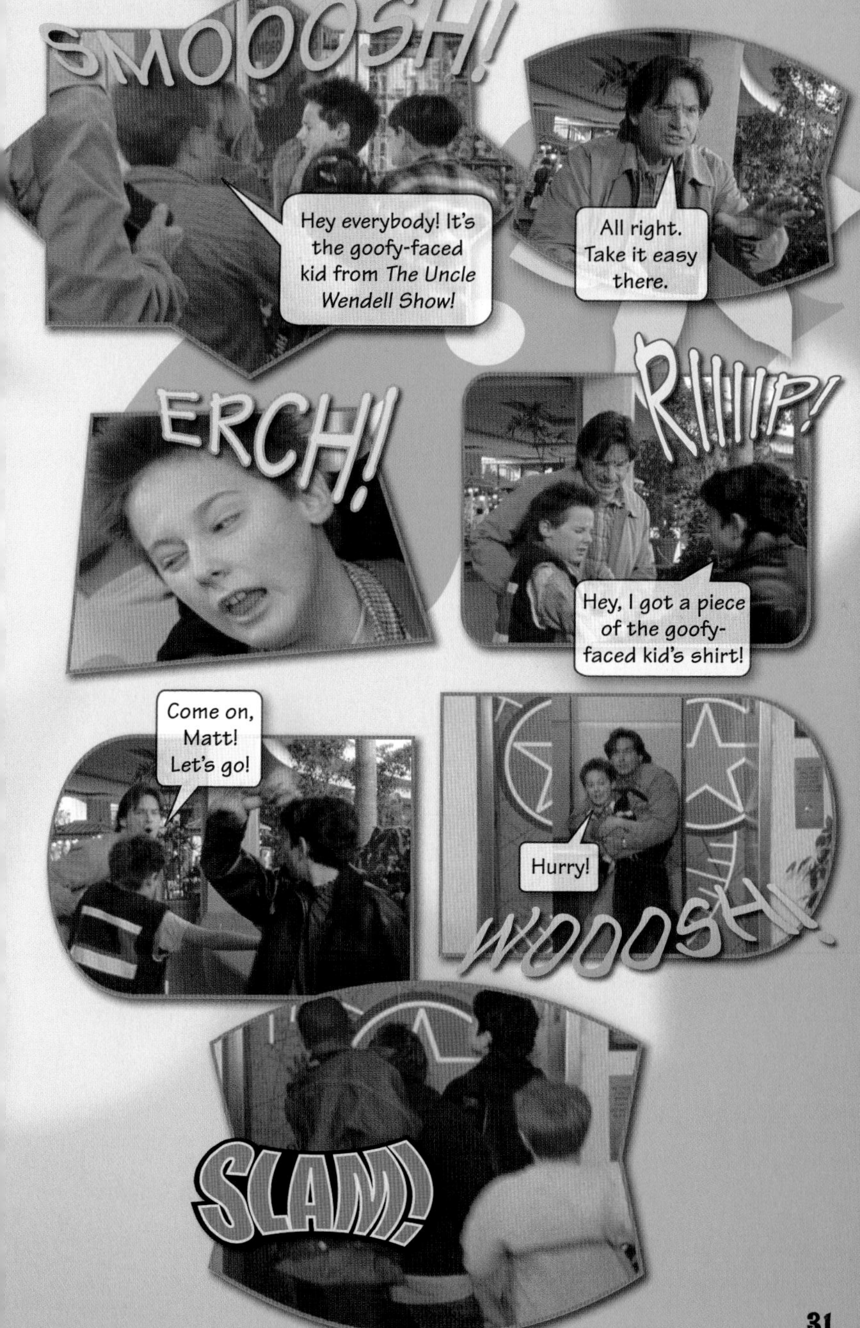
SMOOOSH!
Hey everybody! It's the goofy-faced kid from The Uncle Wendell Show!
All right. Take it easy there.
ERCH!
RIIIIP!
Hey, I got a piece of the goofy-faced kid's shirt!
Come on, Matt! Let's go!
Hurry!
WOOOSH!
SLAM!

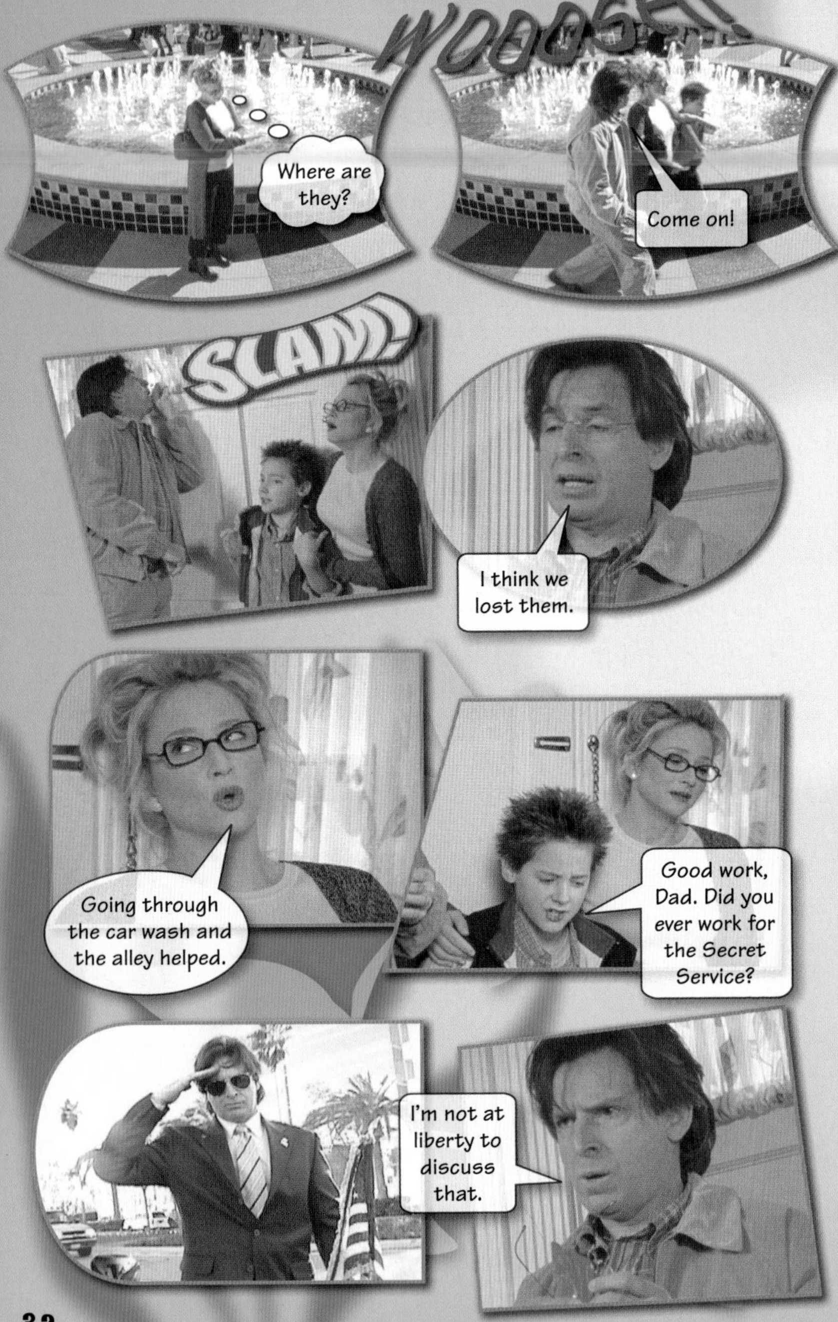
Where are they?
WOOOSH!!
Come on!
SLAM!
I think we lost them.
Going through the car wash and the alley helped.
Good work, Dad. Did you ever work for the Secret Service?
I'm not at liberty to discuss that.

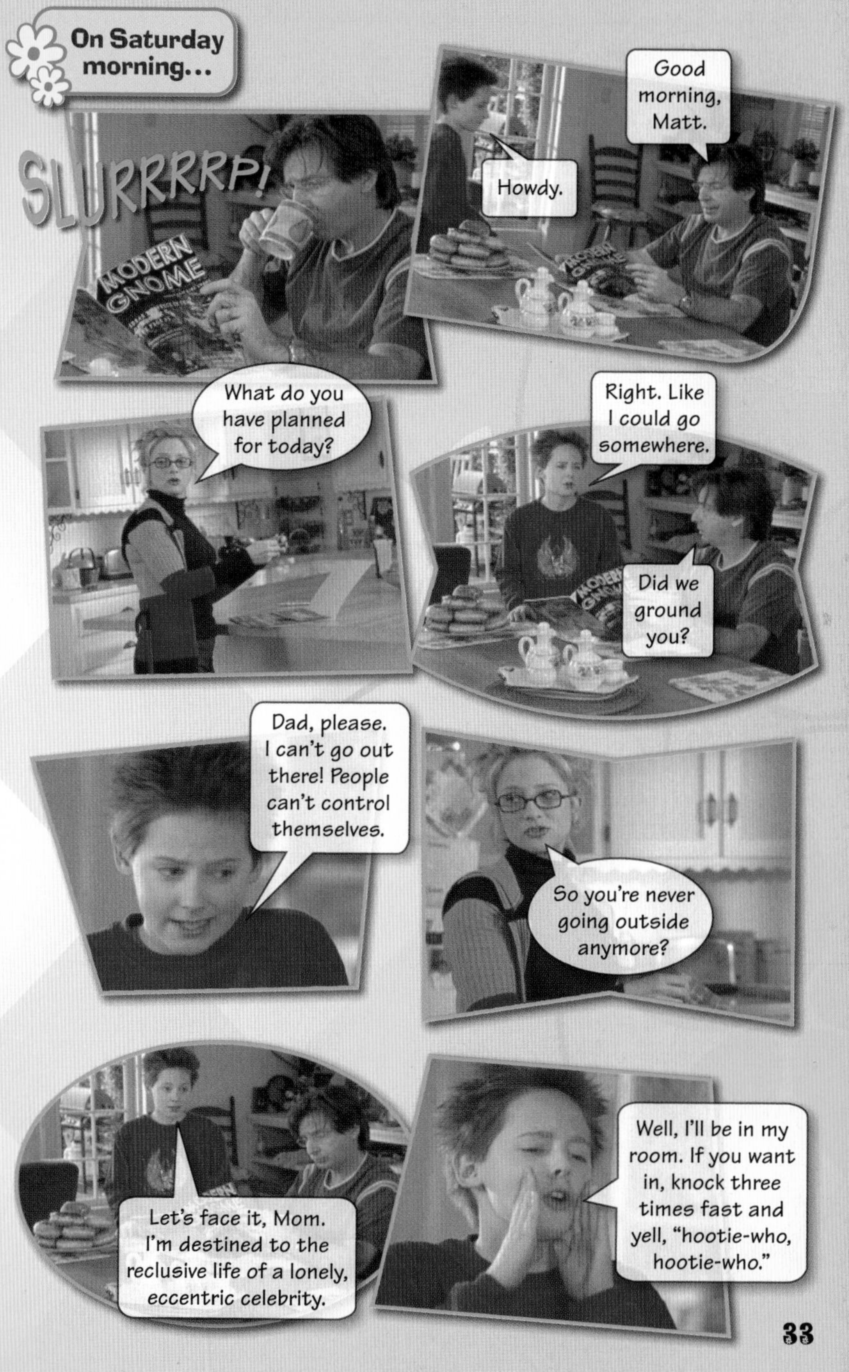

On Saturday morning...
SLURRRRP!
Good morning, Matt.
Howdy.
What do you have planned for today?
Right. Like I could go somewhere.
Did we ground you?
Dad, please. I can't go out there! People can't control themselves.
So you're never going outside anymore?
Let's face it, Mom. I'm destined to the reclusive life of a lonely, eccentric celebrity.
Well, I'll be in my room. If you want in, knock three times fast and yell, "hootie-who, hootie-who."

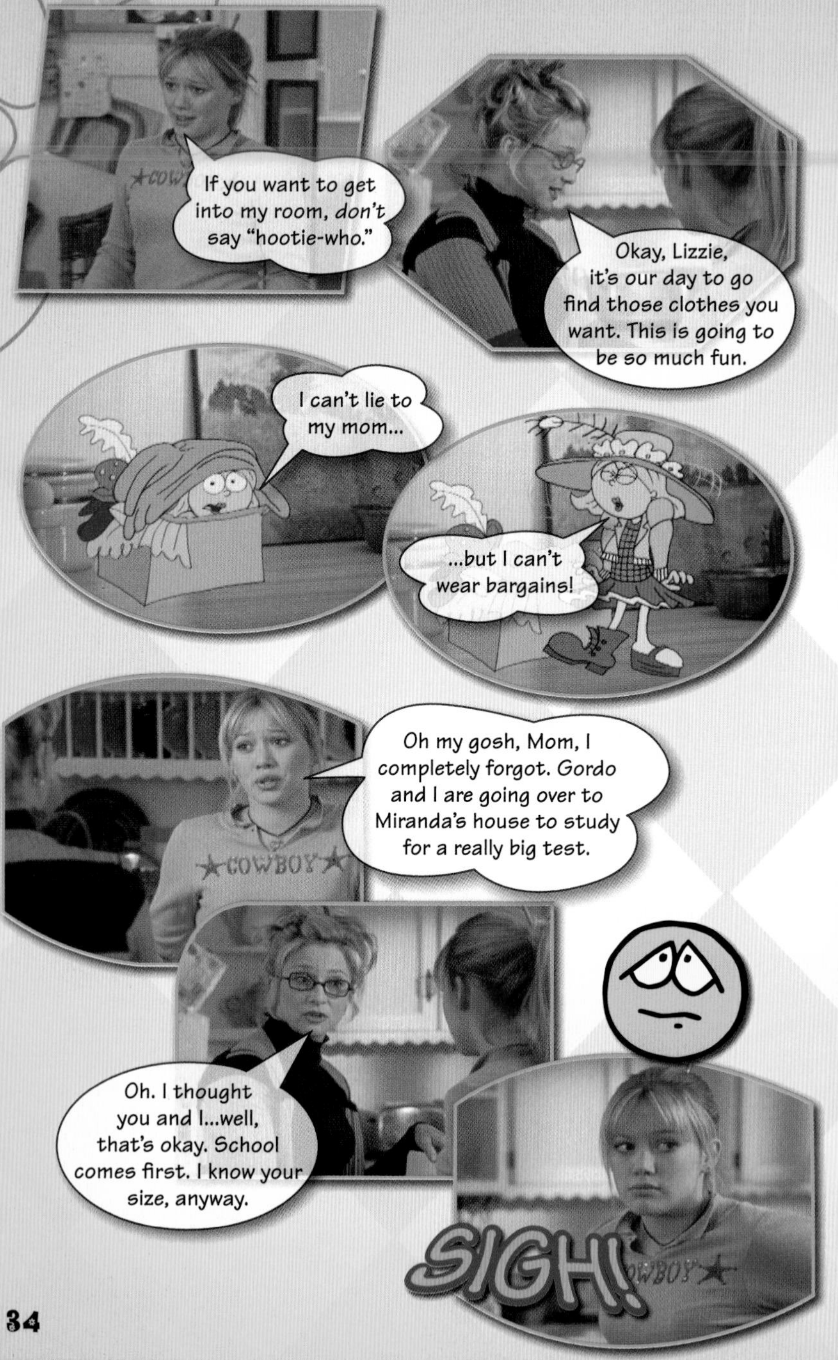

If you want to get into my room, *don't* say "hootie-who."
Okay, Lizzie, it's our day to go find those clothes you want. This is going to be so much fun.
I can't lie to my mom...
...but I can't wear bargains!
Oh my gosh, Mom, I completely forgot. Gordo and I are going over to Miranda's house to study for a really big test.
Oh. I thought you and I...well, that's okay. School comes first. I know your size, anyway.
SIGH!

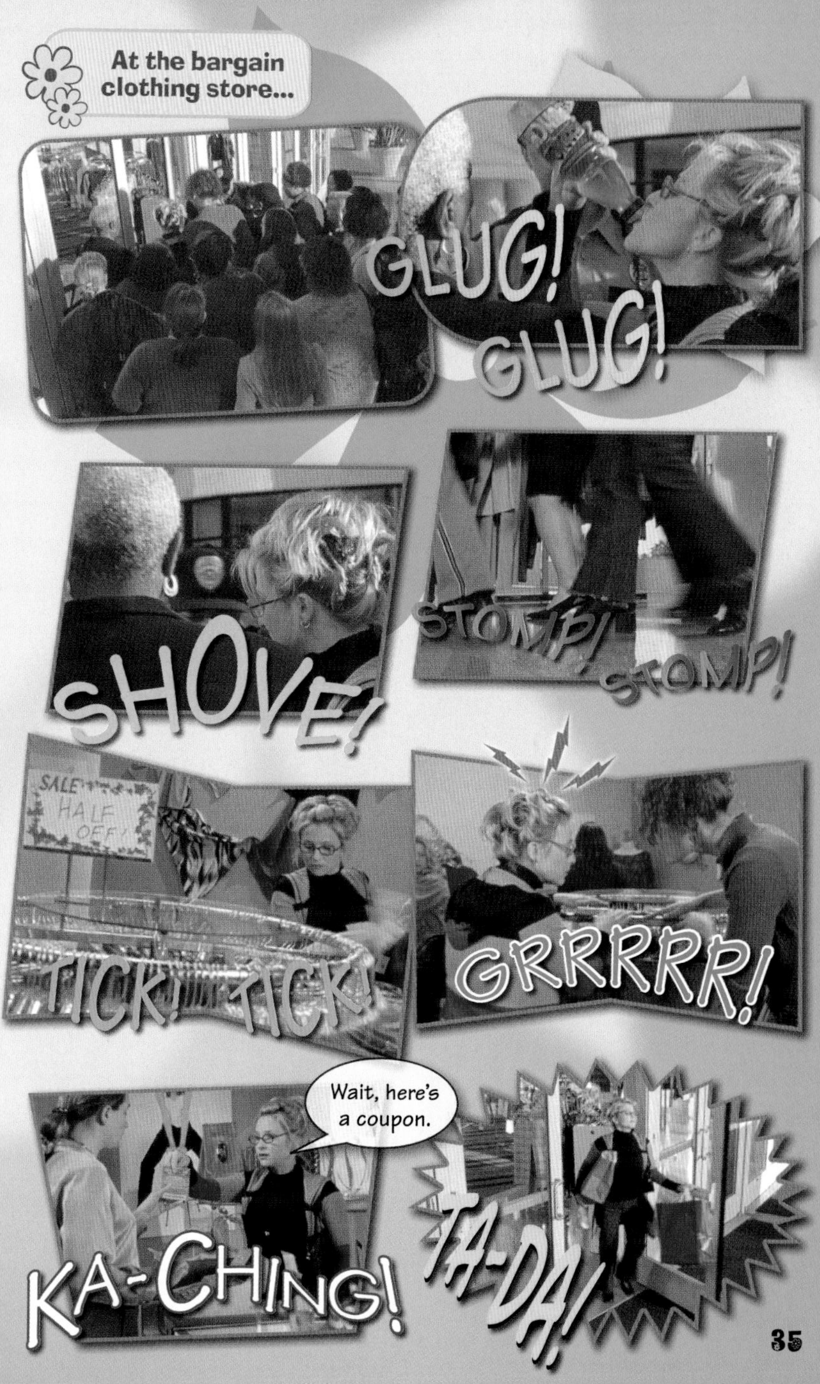
At the bargain clothing store...
GLUG! GLUG!
SHOVE!
STOMP! STOMP!
SALE HALF OFF!
TICK! TICK!
GRRRRR!
Wait, here's a coupon.
KA-CHING!
TA-DA!

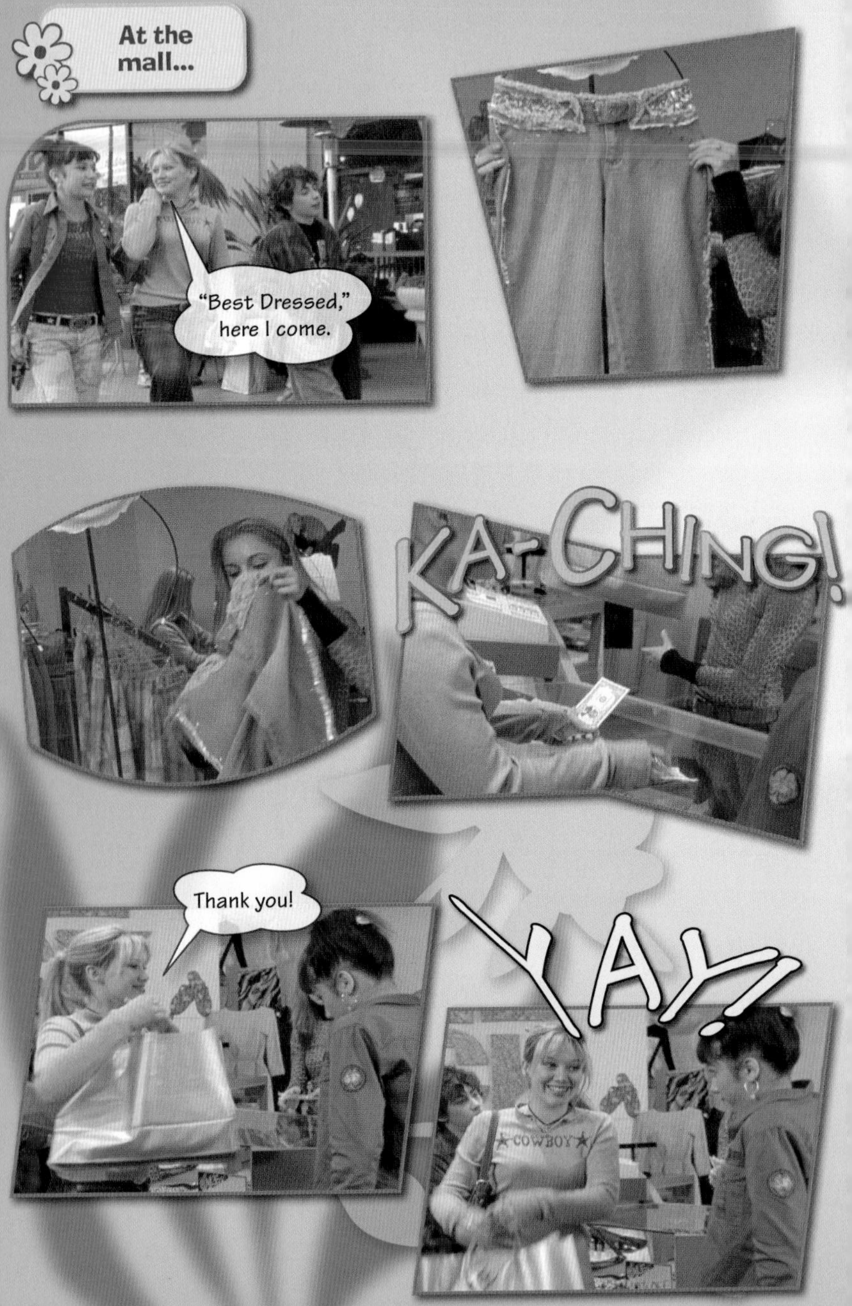
At the mall...
"Best Dressed," here I come.
KA-CHING!
Thank you!
YAY!

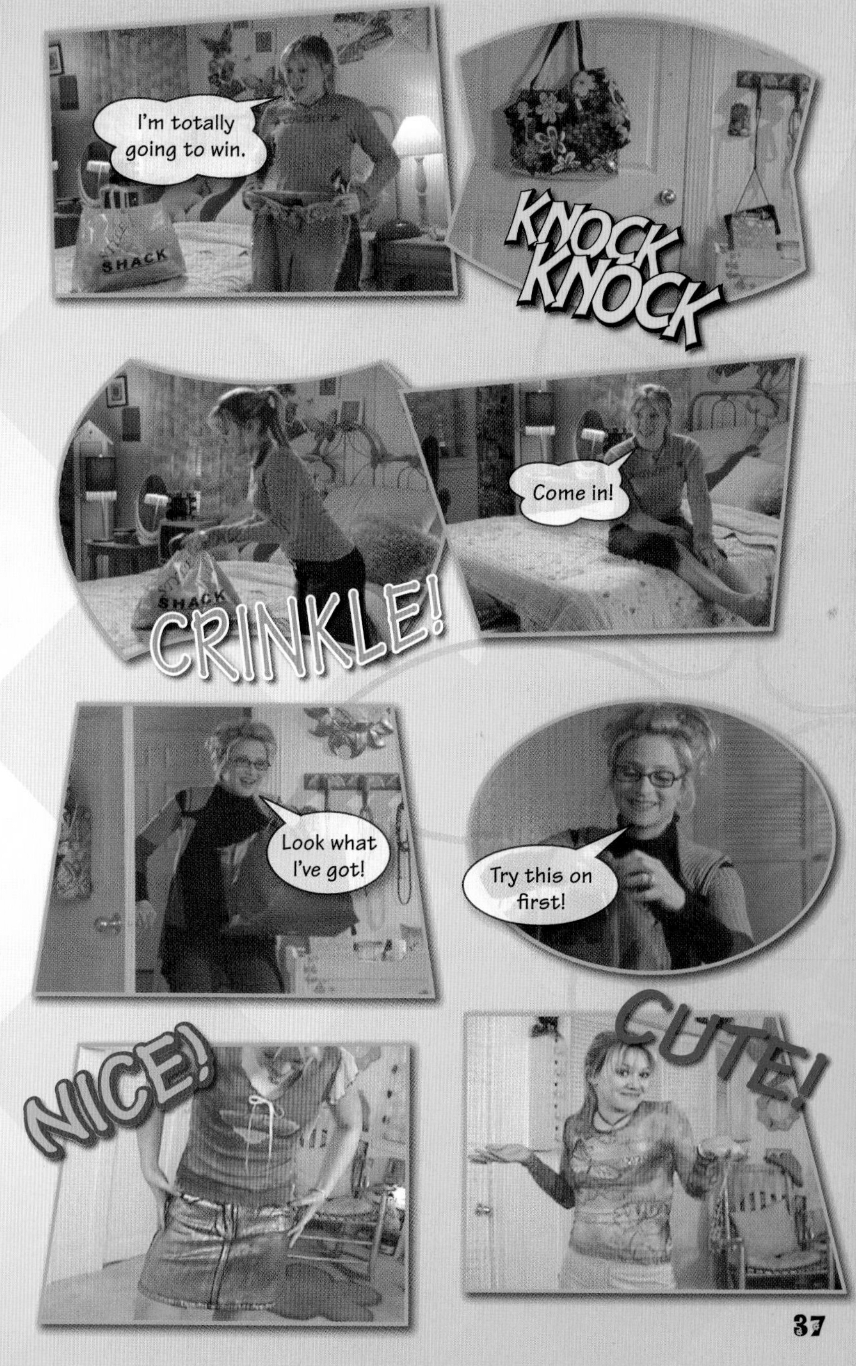
I'm totally going to win.
SHACK
KNOCK KNOCK
SHACK
CRINKLE!
Come in!
Look what I've got!
Try this on first!
NICE!
CUTE!

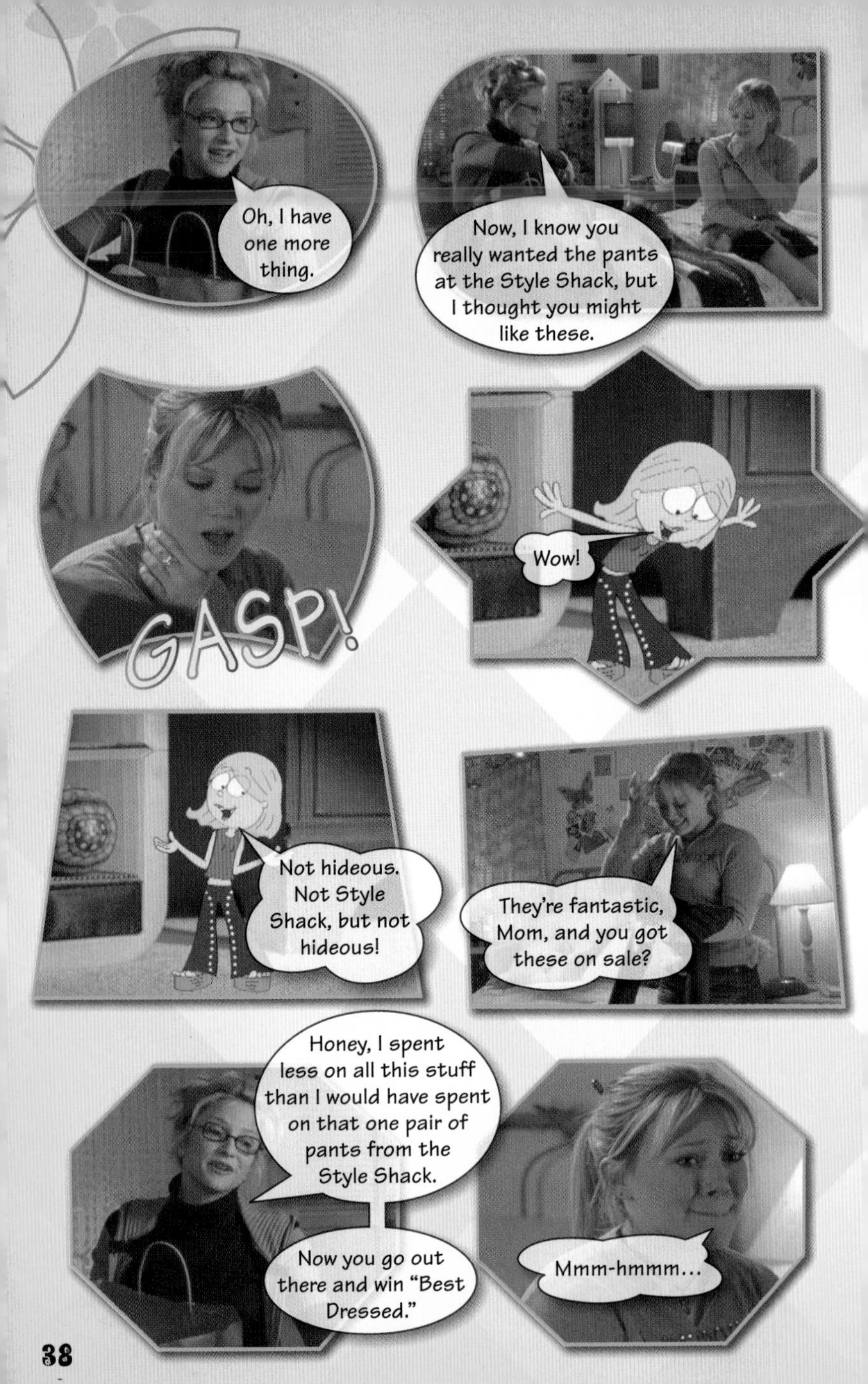
Oh, I have one more thing.
Now, I know you really wanted the pants at the Style Shack, but I thought you might like these.
GASP!
Wow!
Not hideous. Not Style Shack, but not hideous!
They're fantastic, Mom, and you got these on sale?
Honey, I spent less on all this stuff than I would have spent on that one pair of pants from the Style Shack.
Now you go out there and win "Best Dressed."
Mmm-hmmm...

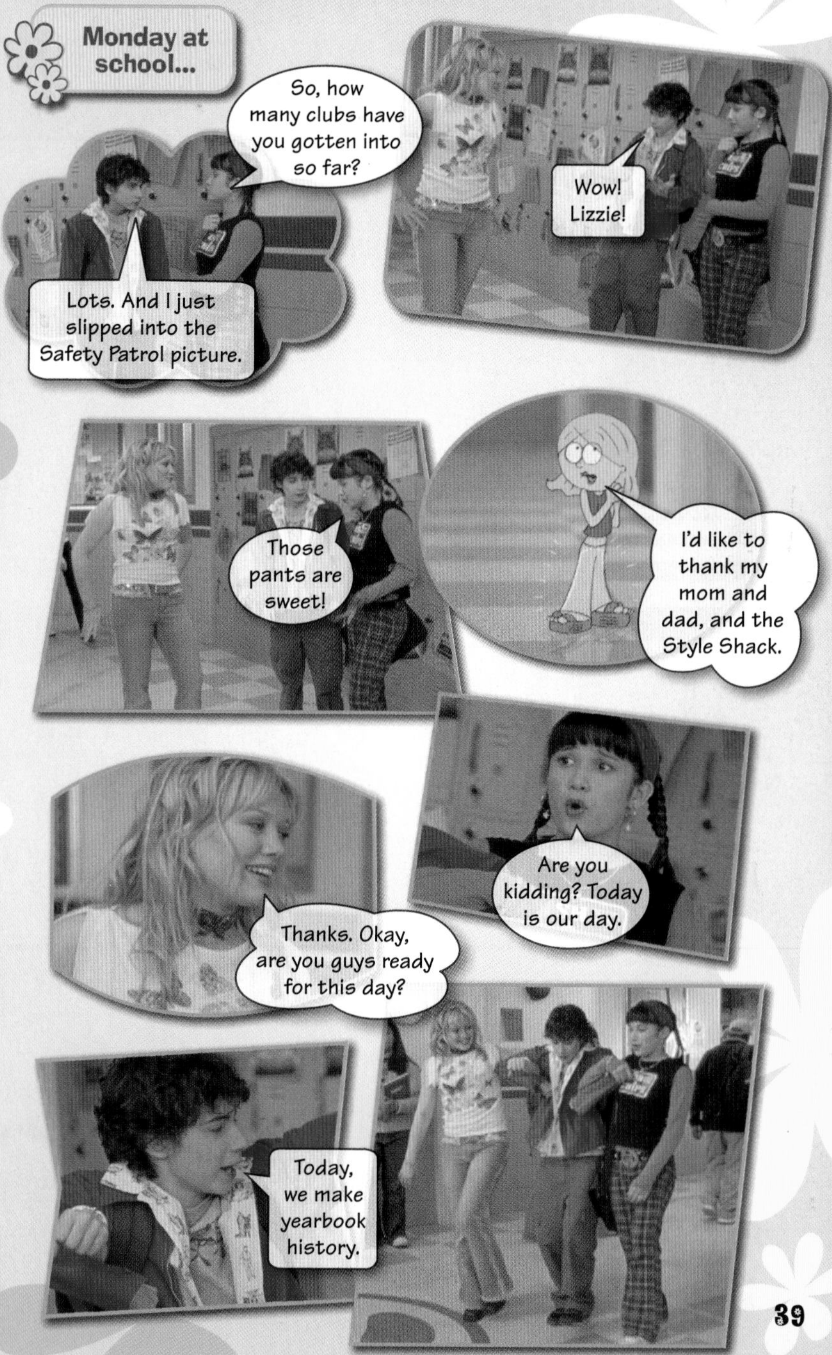
Monday at school...
So, how many clubs have you gotten into so far?
Lots. And I just slipped into the Safety Patrol picture.
Wow! Lizzie!
Those pants are sweet!
I'd like to thank my mom and dad, and the Style Shack.
Thanks. Okay, are you guys ready for this day?
Are you kidding? Today is our day.
Today, we make yearbook history.

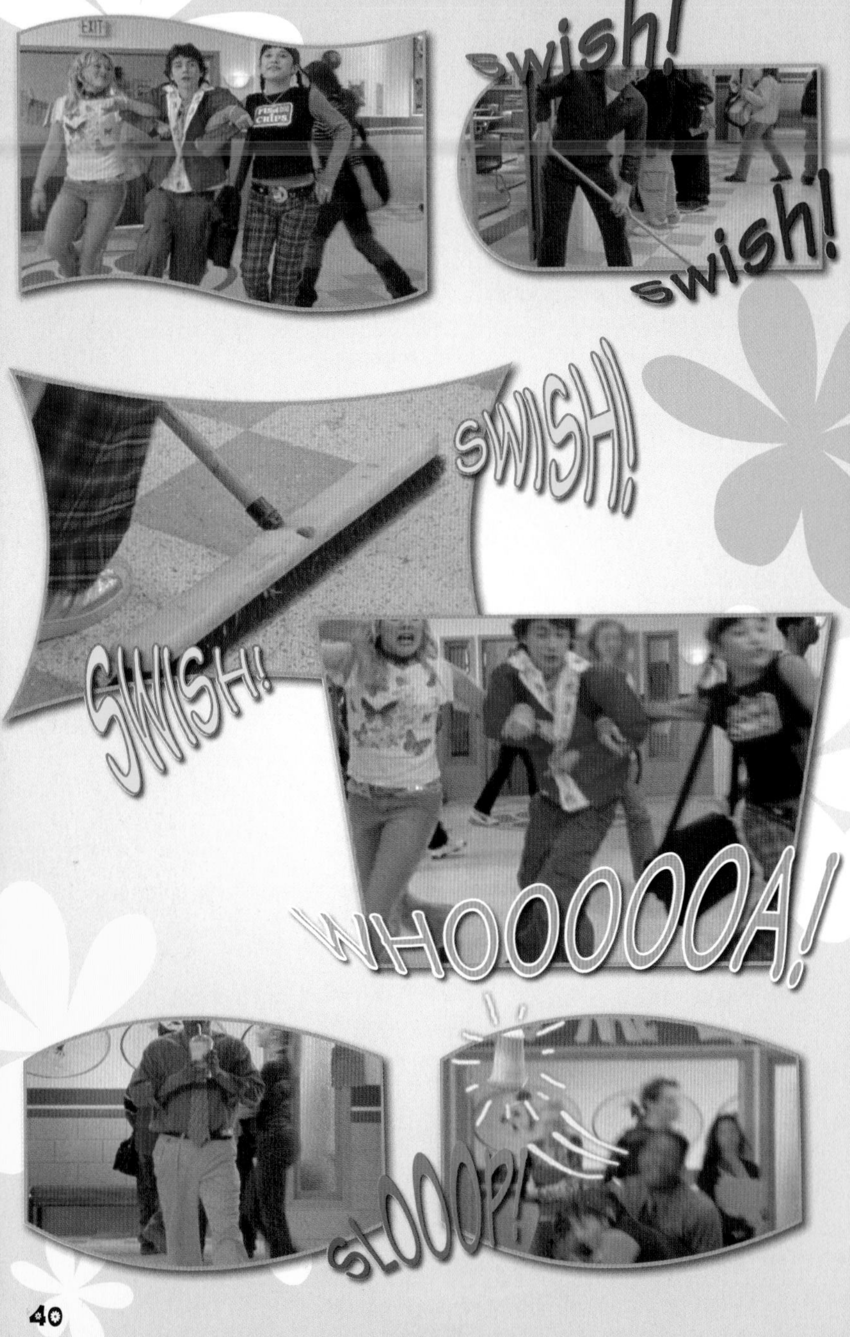
EXIT
swish!
swish!
SWISH!
SWISH!
WHOOOOOA!
SLOOOP!

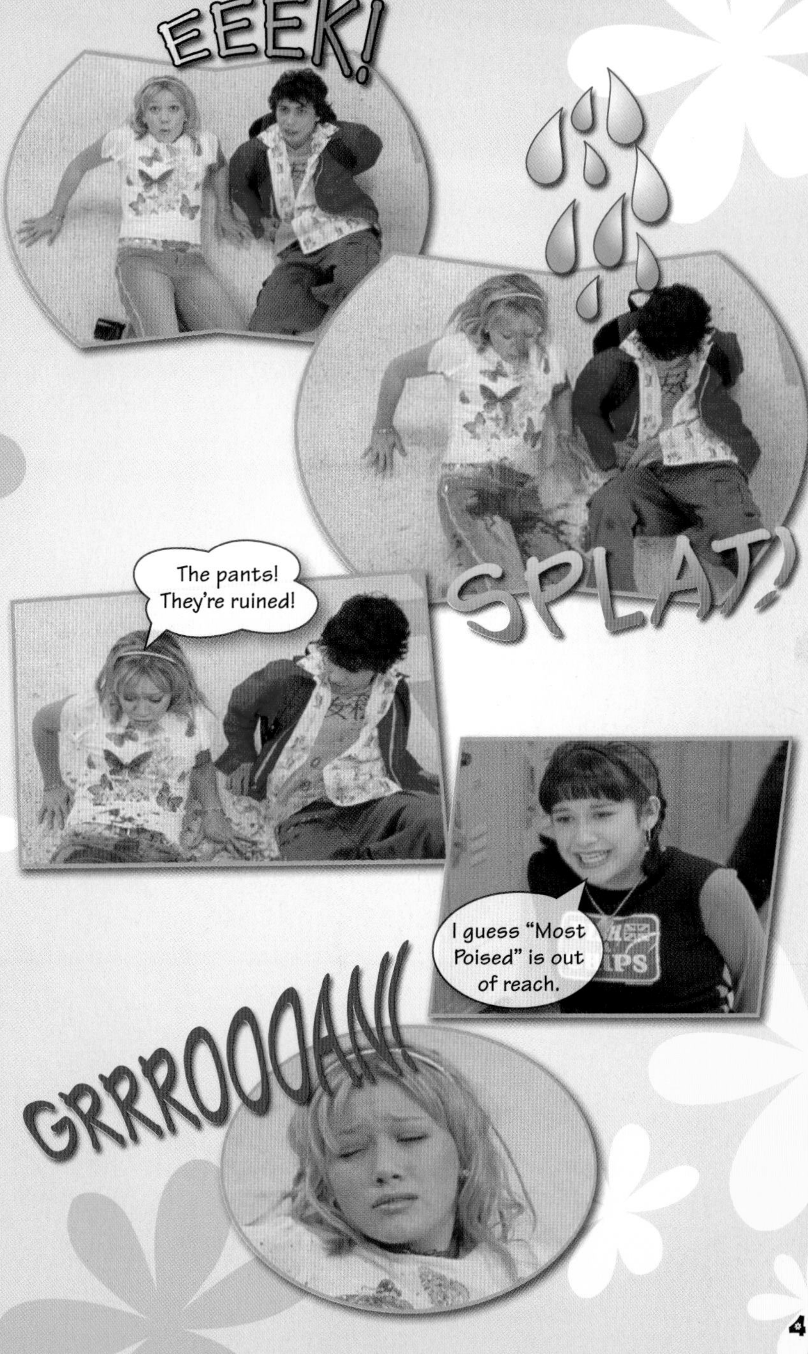
EEEK!
SPLAT!
The pants! They're ruined!
I guess "Most Poised" is out of reach.
GRRROOOAN!

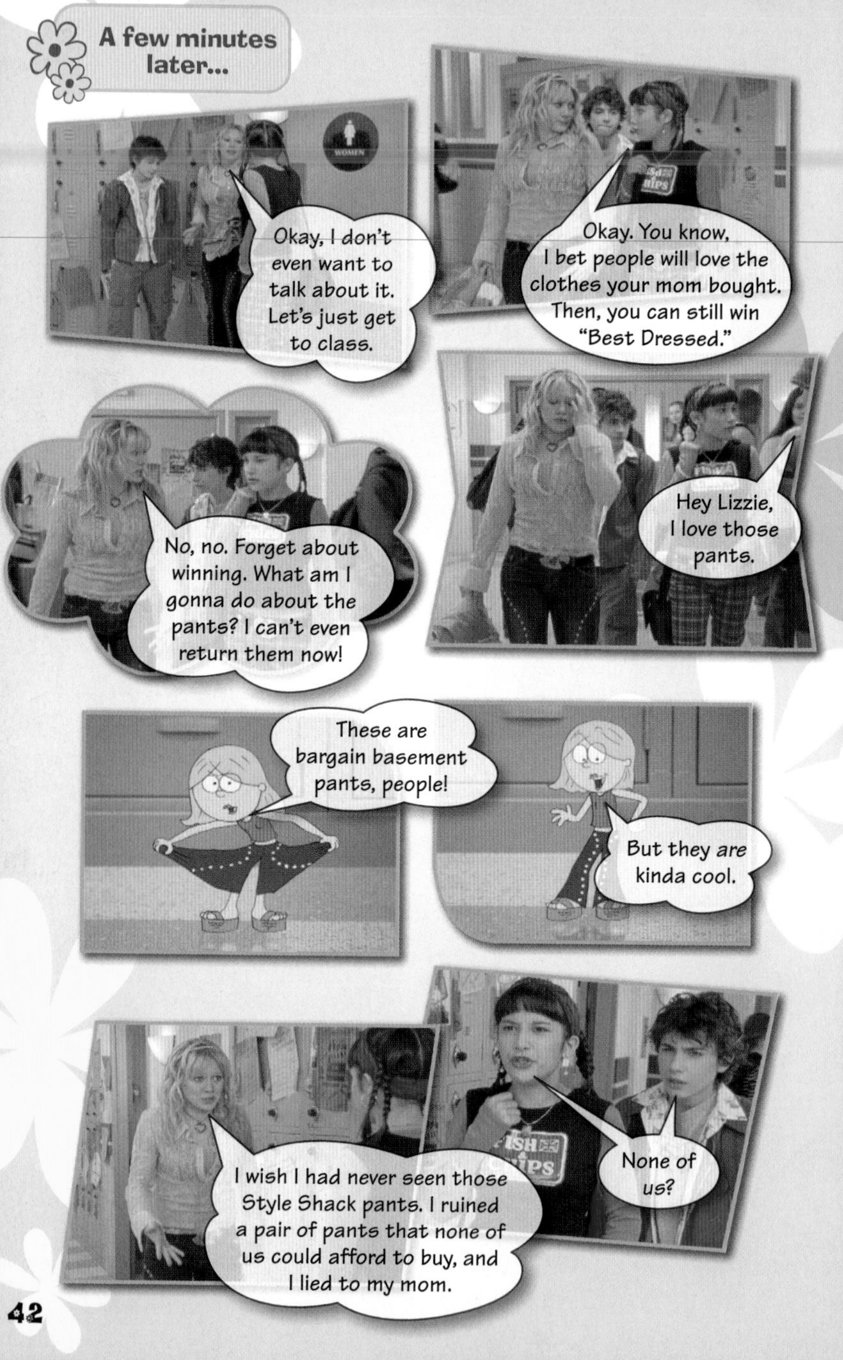
A few minutes later...
Okay, I don't even want to talk about it. Let's just get to class.
Okay. You know, I bet people will love the clothes your mom bought. Then, you can still win "Best Dressed."
No, no. Forget about winning. What am I gonna do about the pants? I can't even return them now!
Hey Lizzie, I love those pants.
These are bargain basement pants, people!
But they are kinda cool.
I wish I had never seen those Style Shack pants. I ruined a pair of pants that none of us could afford to buy, and I lied to my mom.
None of us?

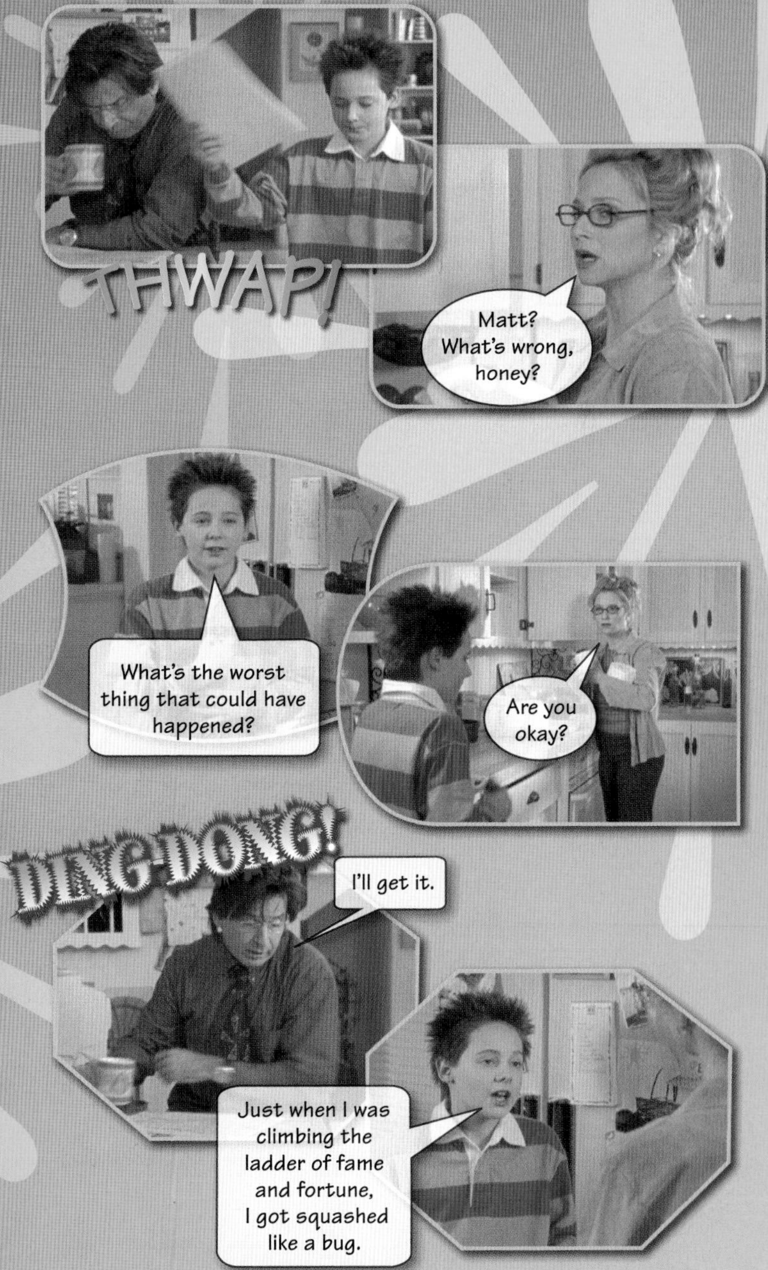

THWAP!
Matt? What's wrong, honey?
What's the worst thing that could have happened?
Are you okay?
DING-DONG!
I'll get it.
Just when I was climbing the ladder of fame and fortune, I got squashed like a bug.

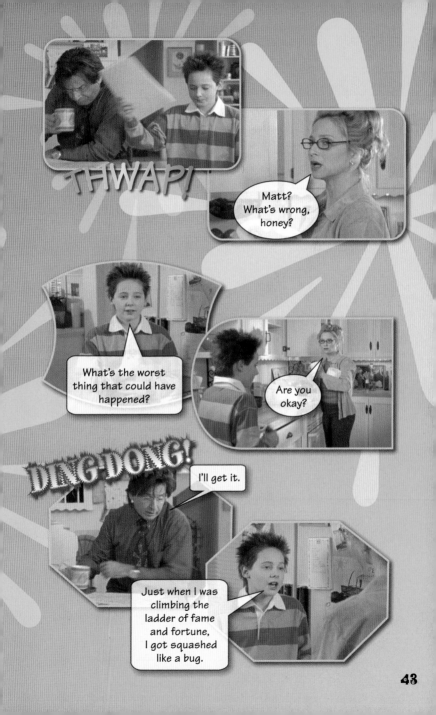

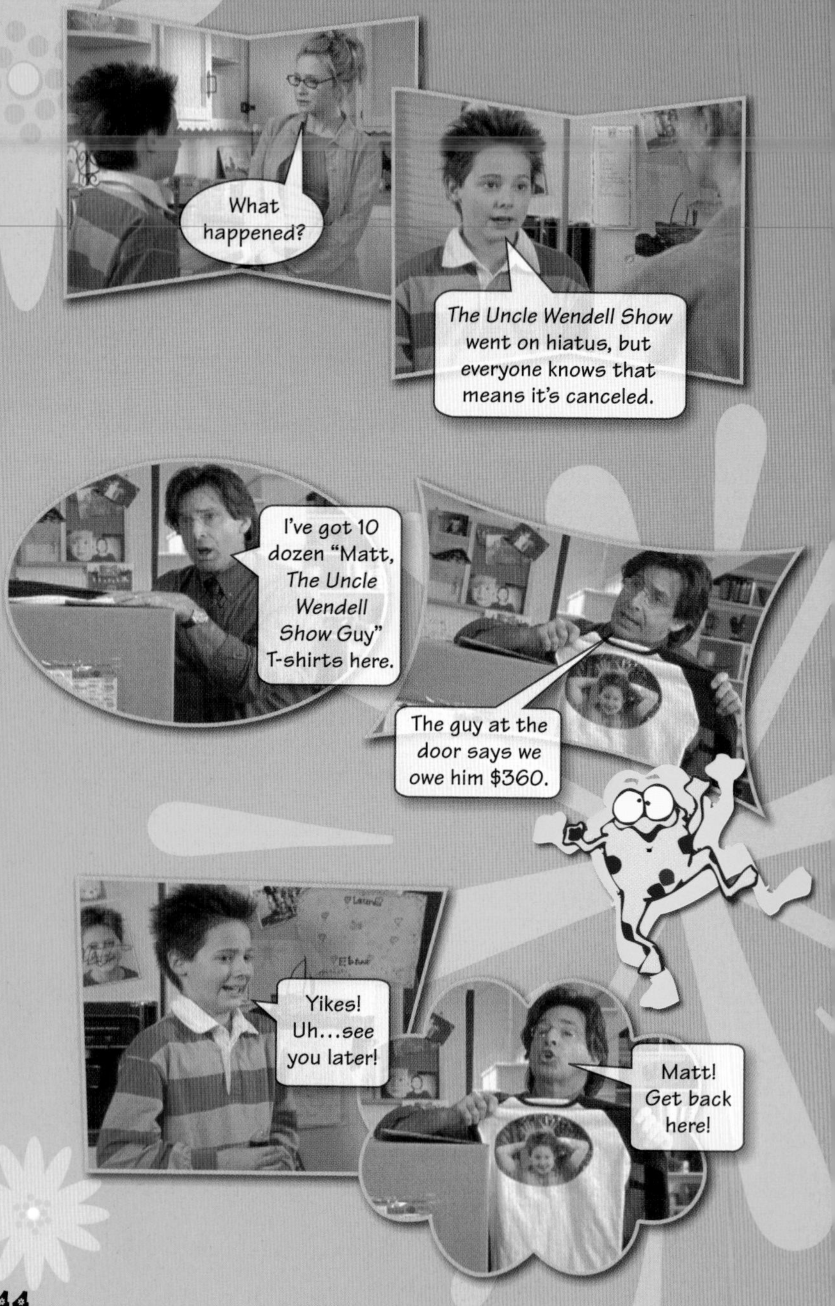

What happened?
The Uncle Wendell Show went on hiatus, but everyone knows that means it's canceled.
I've got 10 dozen "Matt, *The Uncle Wendell Show* Guy" T-shirts here.
The guy at the door says we owe him $360.
Yikes! Uh...see you later!
Matt! Get back here!

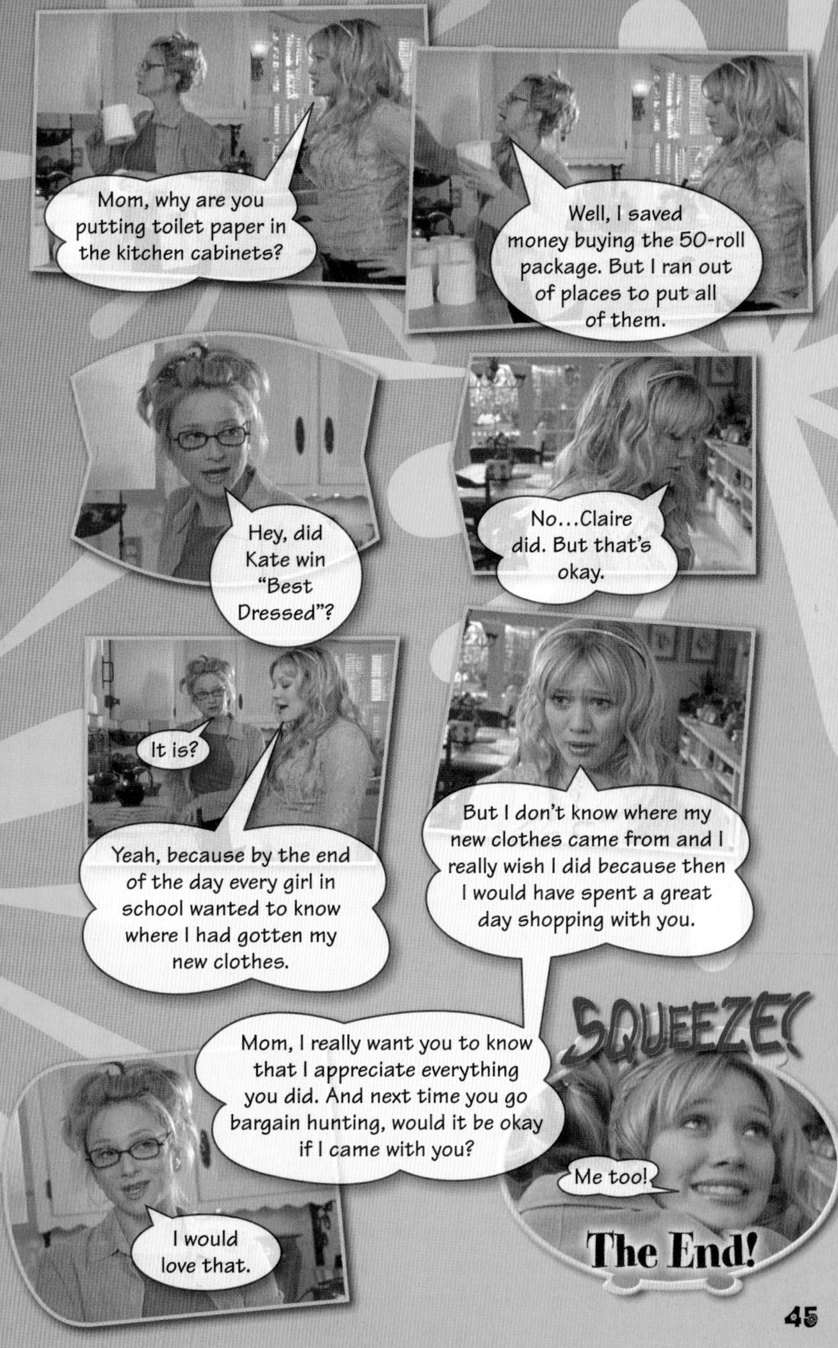
Mom, why are you putting toilet paper in the kitchen cabinets?
Well, I saved money buying the 50-roll package. But I ran out of places to put all of them.
Hey, did Kate win "Best Dressed"?
No...Claire did. But that's okay.
It is?
Yeah, because by the end of the day every girl in school wanted to know where I had gotten my new clothes.
But I don't know where my new clothes came from and I really wish I did because then I would have spent a great day shopping with you.
Mom, I really want you to know that I appreciate everything you did. And next time you go bargain hunting, would it be okay if I came with you?
I would love that.
SQUEEZE!
Me too!
The End!

Lizzie McGuire

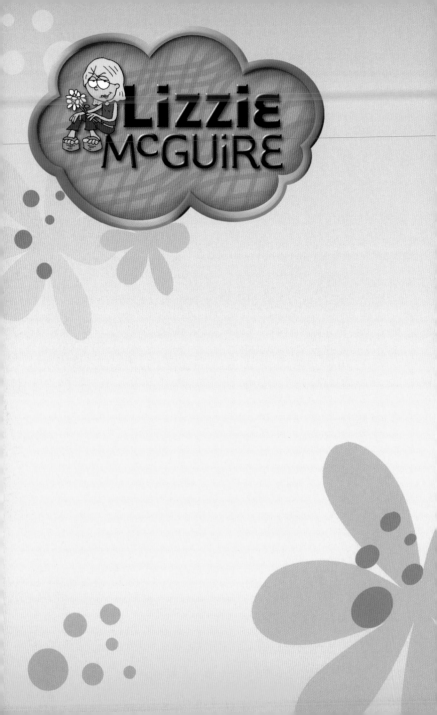

Inner Beauty

When Miranda's diet spins out of control, how can Lizzie and Gordo convince their best friend that she already looks great?

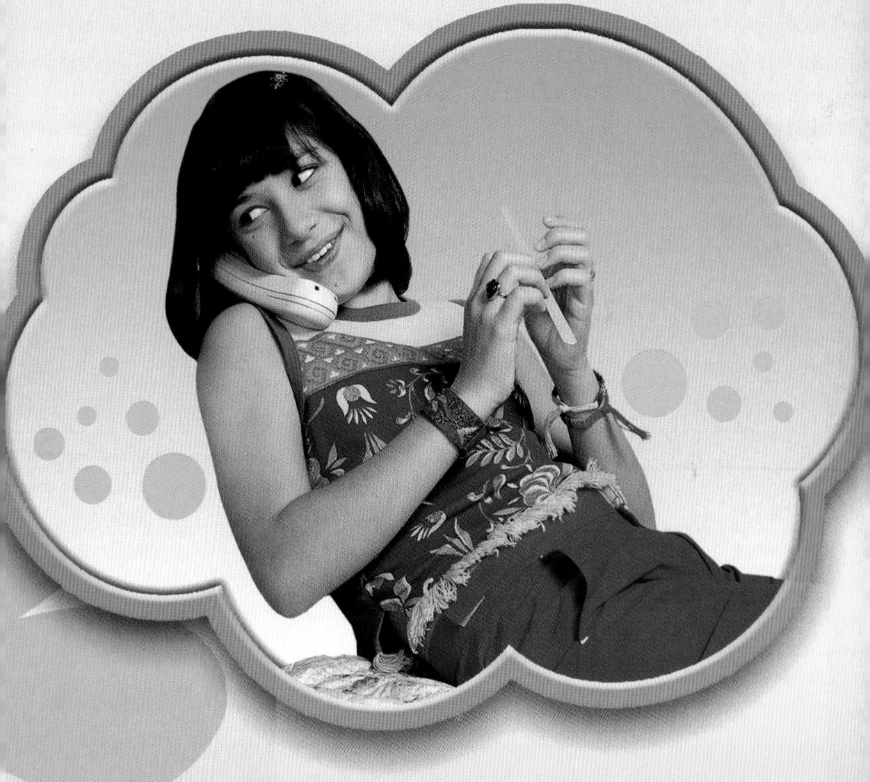

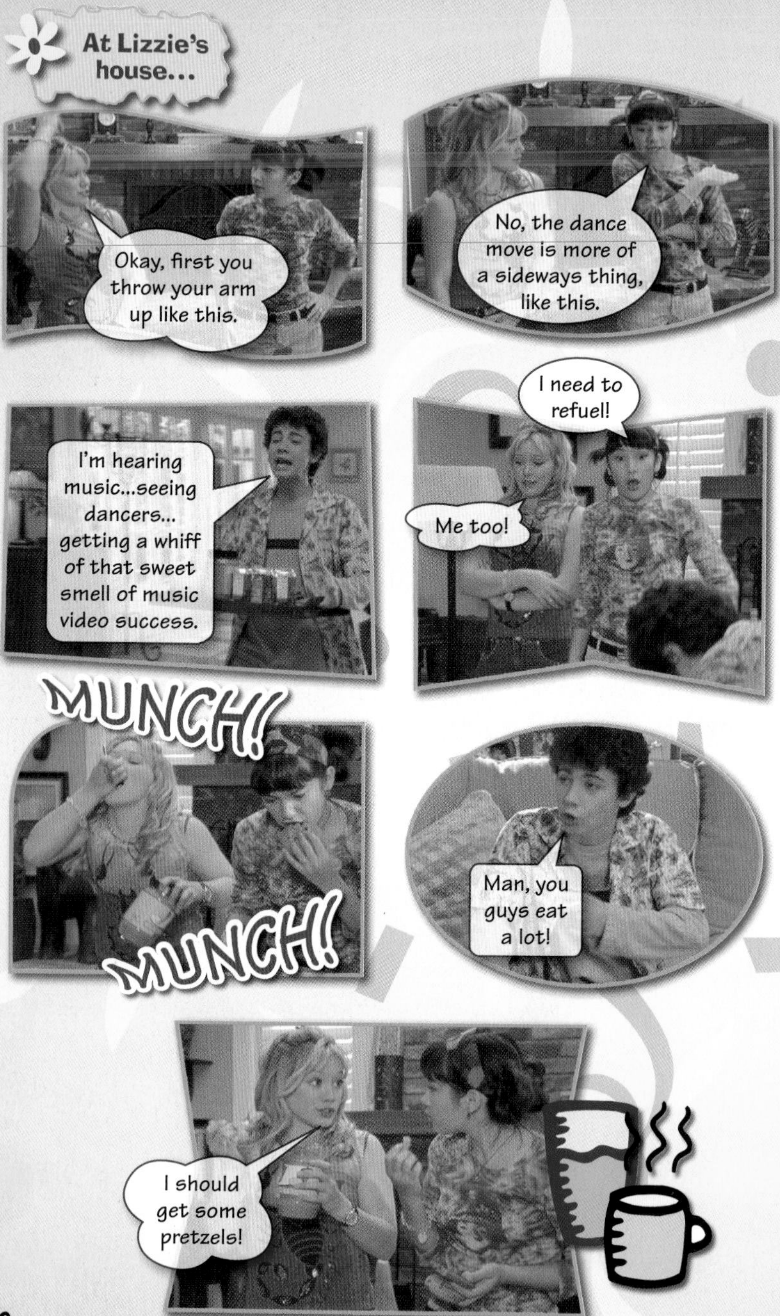

At Lizzie's house...
Okay, first you throw your arm up like this.
No, the dance move is more of a sideways thing, like this.
I'm hearing music...seeing dancers... getting a whiff of that sweet smell of music video success.
I need to refuel!
Me too!
MUNCH!
MUNCH!
Man, you guys eat a lot!
I should get some pretzels!

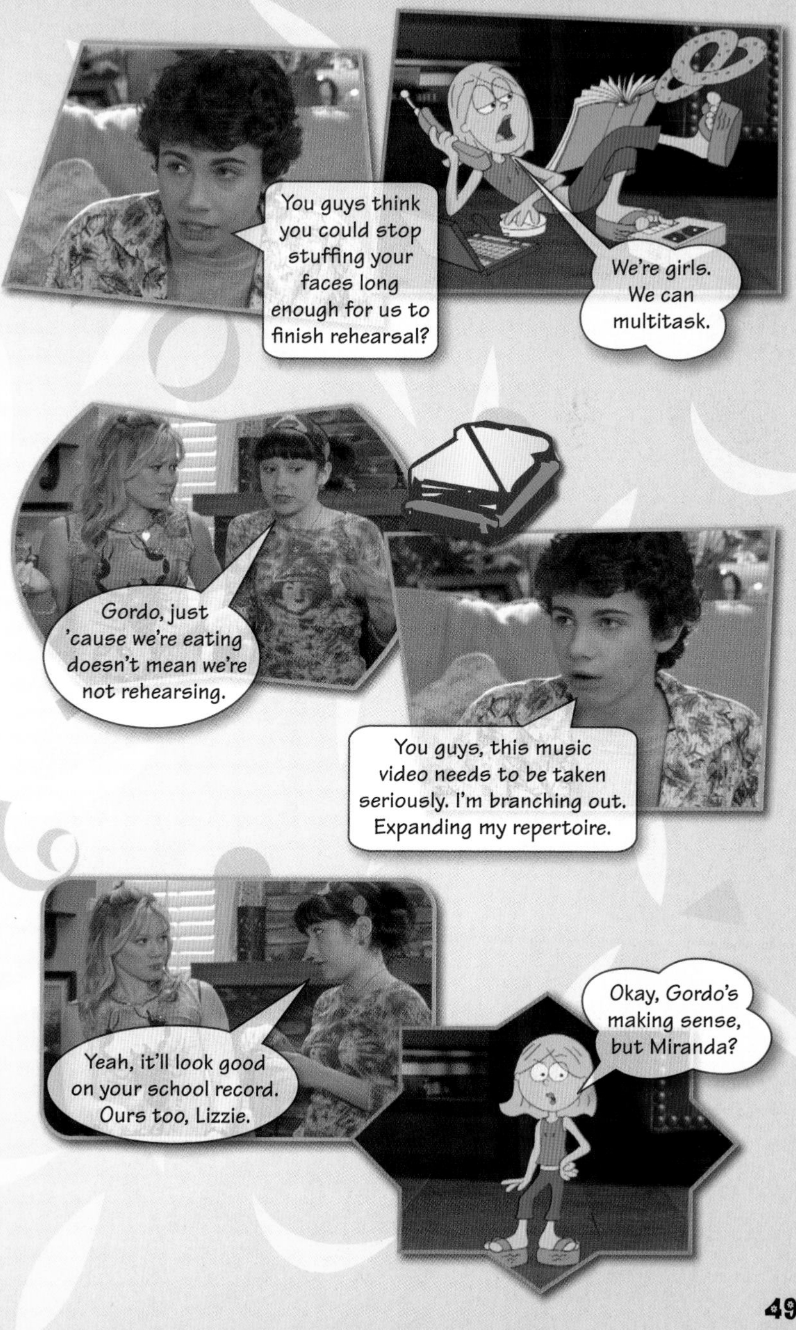
You guys think you could stop stuffing your faces long enough for us to finish rehearsal?
We're girls. We can multitask.
Gordo, just 'cause we're eating doesn't mean we're not rehearsing.
You guys, this music video needs to be taken seriously. I'm branching out. Expanding my repertoire.
Yeah, it'll look good on your school record. Ours too, Lizzie.
Okay, Gordo's making sense, but Miranda?

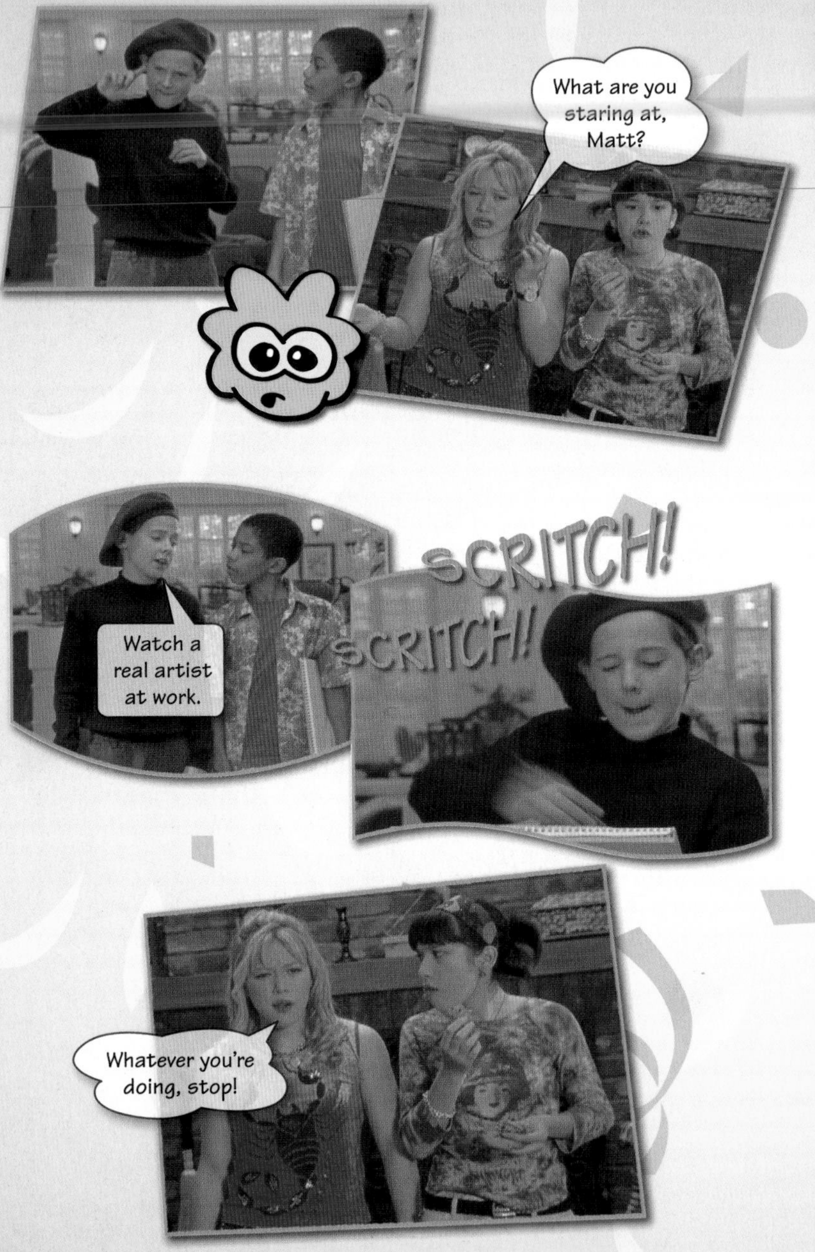
What are you staring at, Matt?
Watch a real artist at work.
SCRITCH!
SCRITCH!
Whatever you're doing, stop!

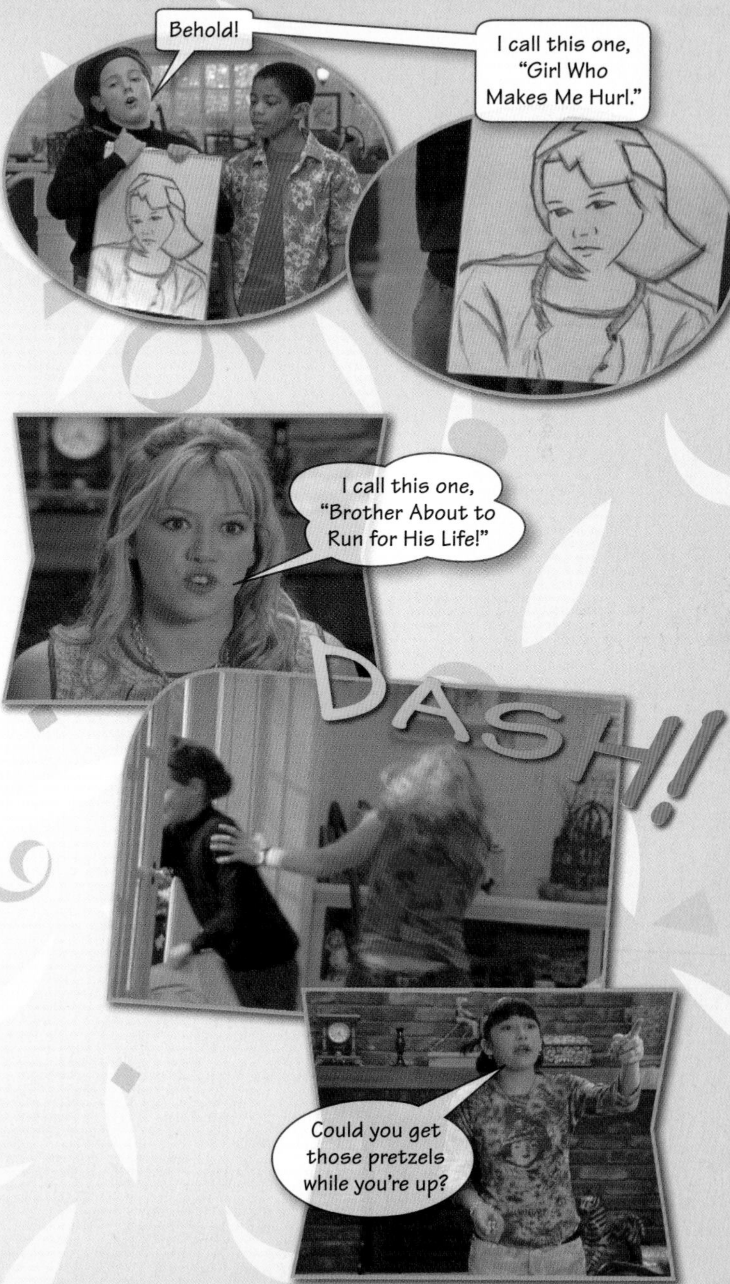
Behold!
I call this one, "Girl Who Makes Me Hurl."
I call this one, "Brother About to Run for His Life!"
DASH!
Could you get those pretzels while you're up?

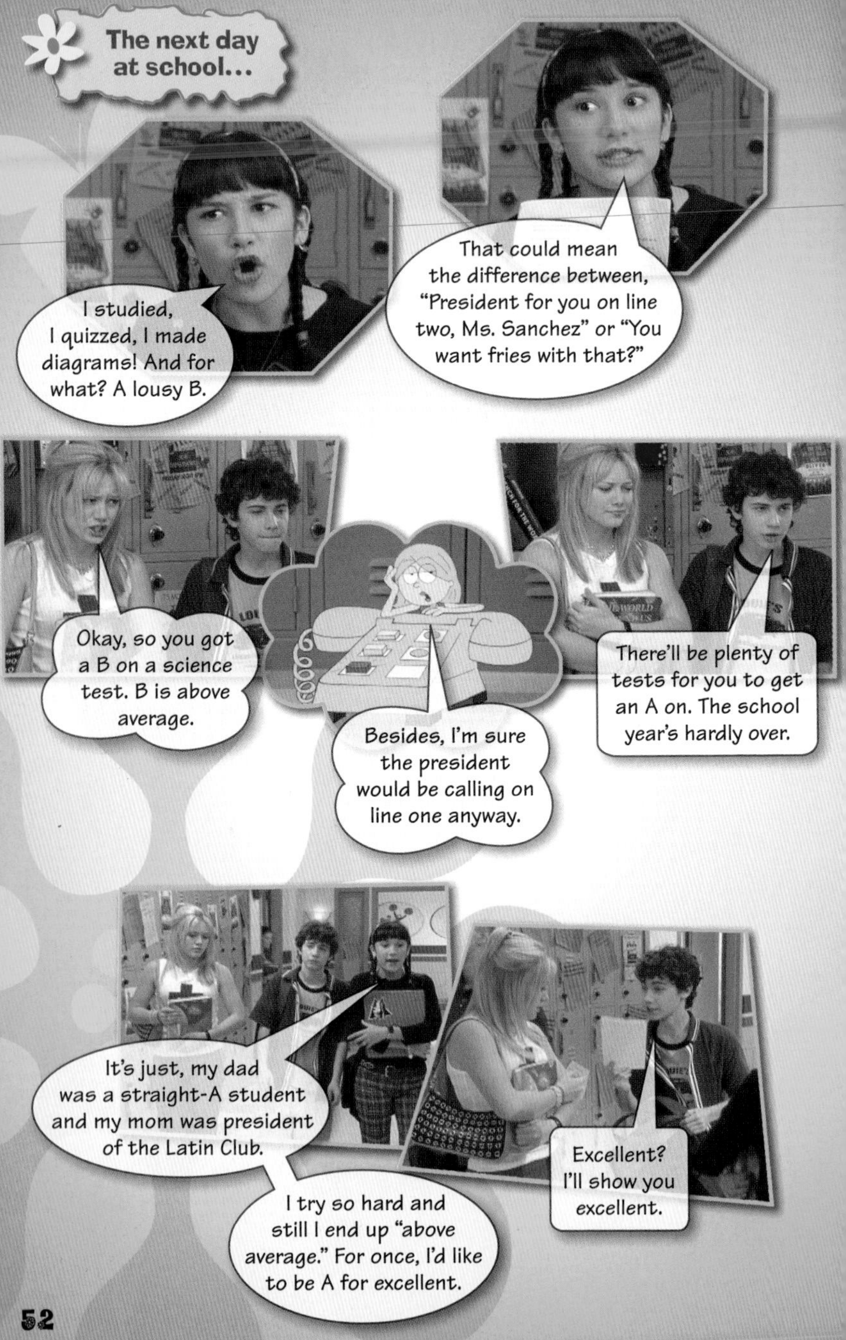
The next day at school...
I studied, I quizzed, I made diagrams! And for what? A lousy B.
That could mean the difference between, "President for you on line two, Ms. Sanchez" or "You want fries with that?"
Okay, so you got a B on a science test. B is above average.
Besides, I'm sure the president would be calling on line one anyway.
There'll be plenty of tests for you to get an A on. The school year's hardly over.
It's just, my dad was a straight-A student and my mom was president of the Latin Club.
I try so hard and still I end up "above average." For once, I'd like to be A for excellent.
Excellent? I'll show you excellent.

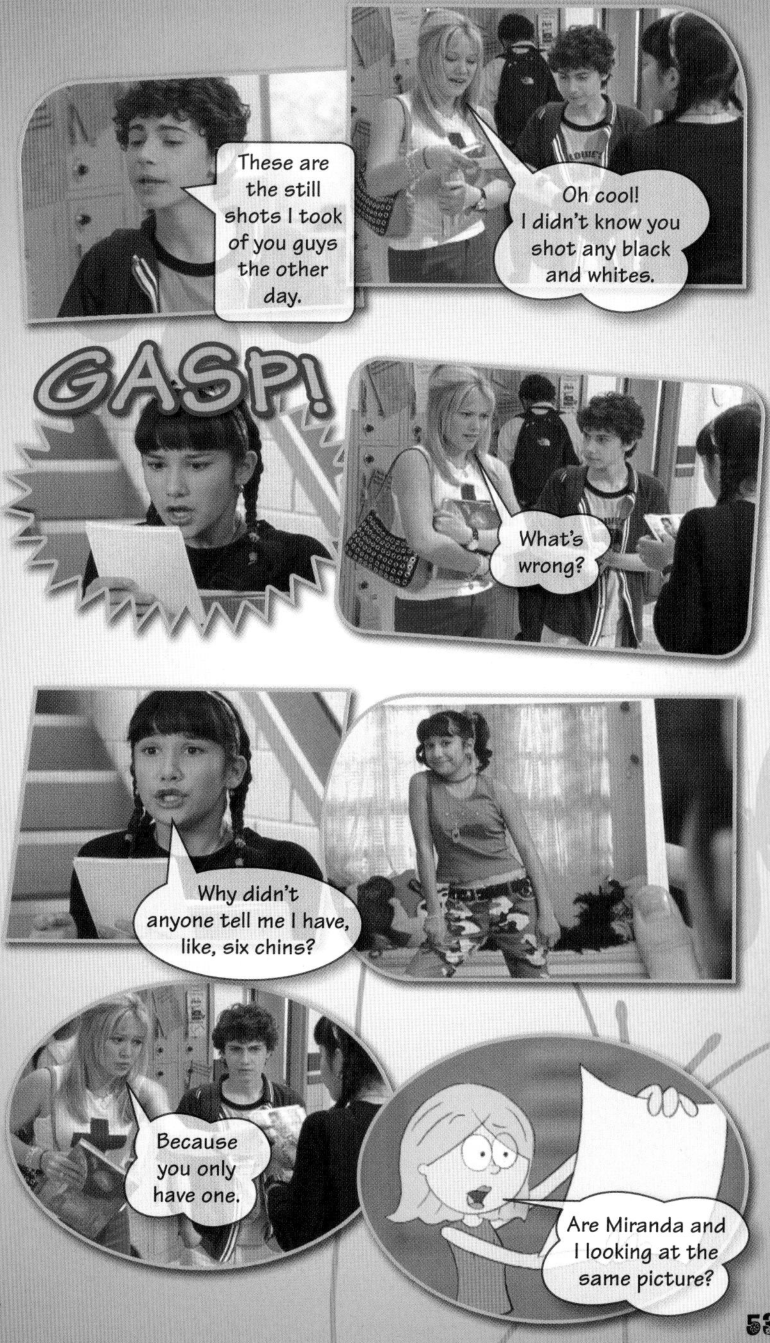
These are the still shots I took of you guys the other day.
Oh cool! I didn't know you shot any black and whites.
GASP!
What's wrong?
Why didn't anyone tell me I have, like, six chins?
Because you only have one.
Are Miranda and I looking at the same picture?

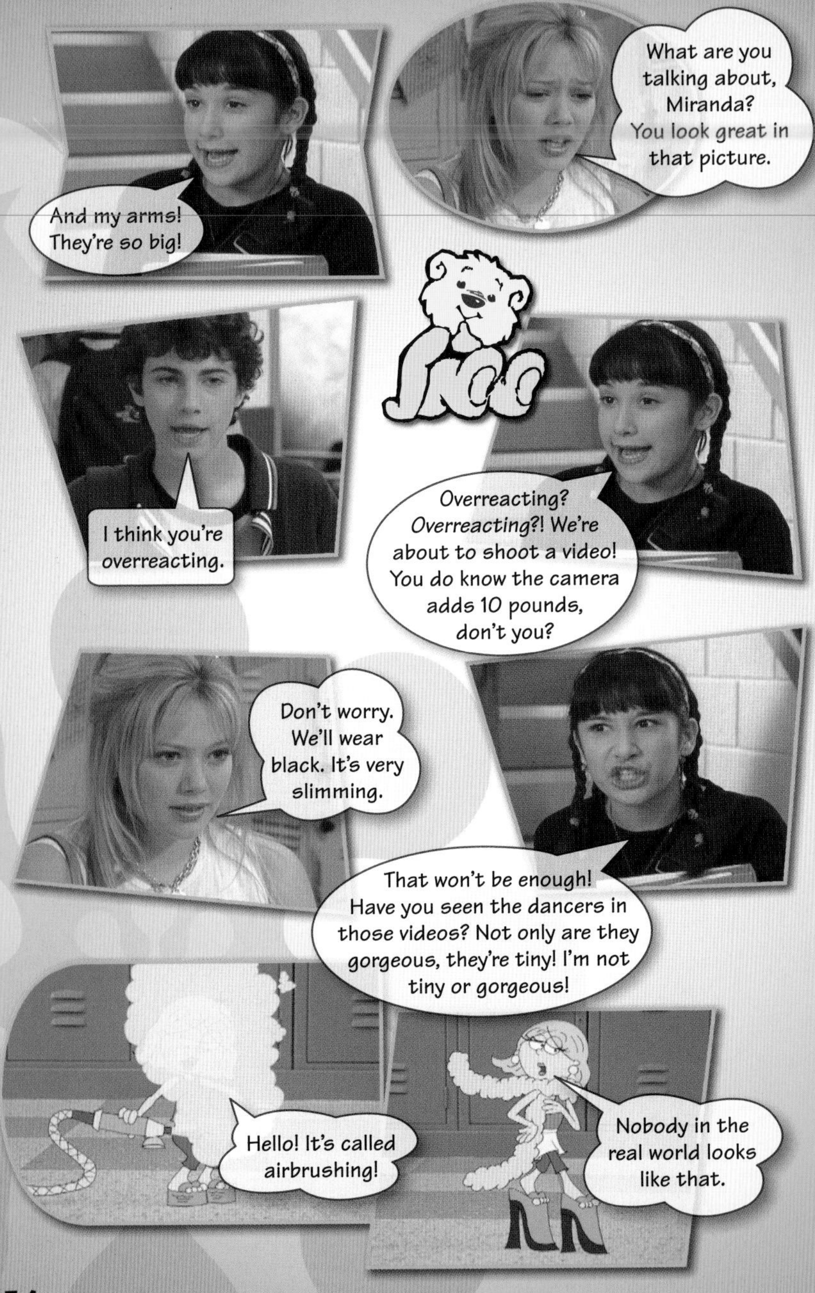
And my arms! They're so big!
What are you talking about, Miranda? You look great in that picture.
I think you're overreacting.
Overreacting? *Overreacting*?! We're about to shoot a video! You do know the camera adds 10 pounds, don't you?
Don't worry. We'll wear black. It's very slimming.
That won't be enough! Have you seen the dancers in those videos? Not only are they gorgeous, they're tiny! I'm not tiny or gorgeous!
Hello! It's called airbrushing!
Nobody in the real world looks like that.

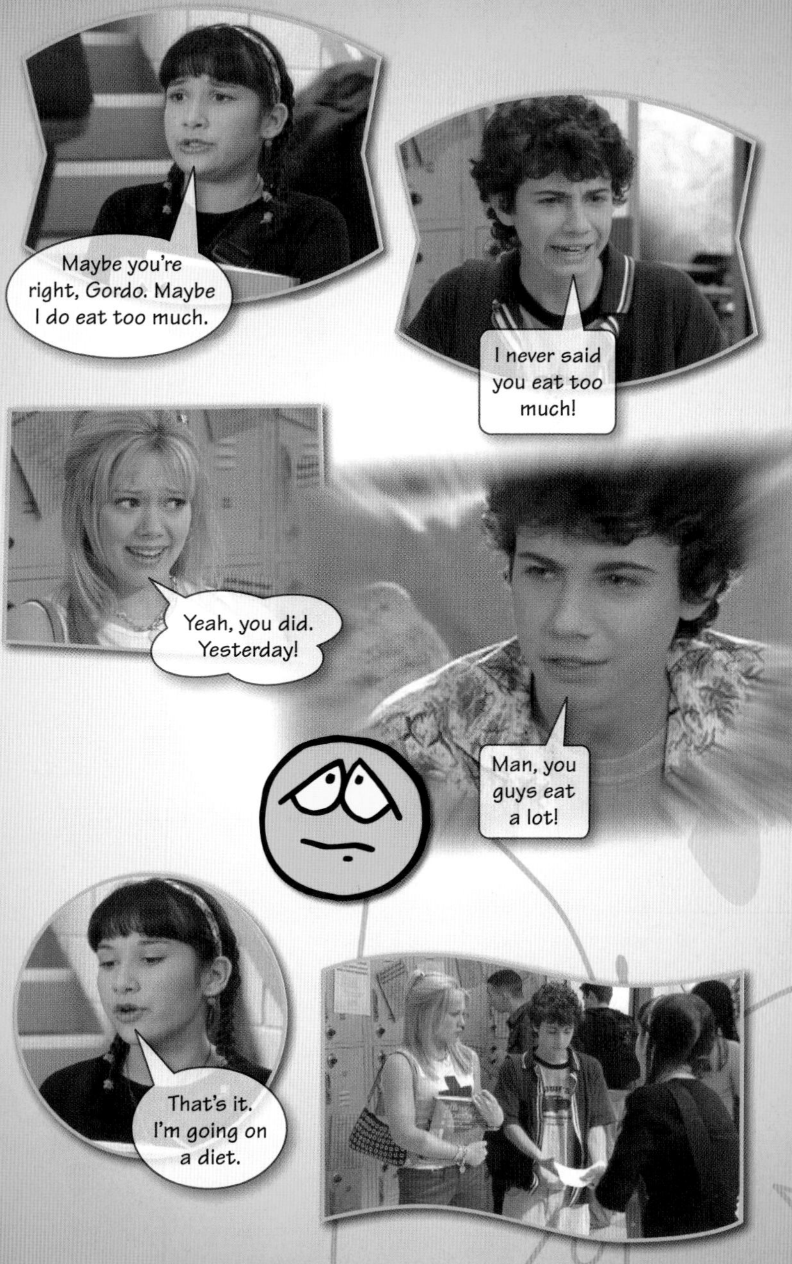
Maybe you're right, Gordo. Maybe I do eat too much.
I never said you eat too much!
Yeah, you did. Yesterday!
Man, you guys eat a lot!
That's it. I'm going on a diet.

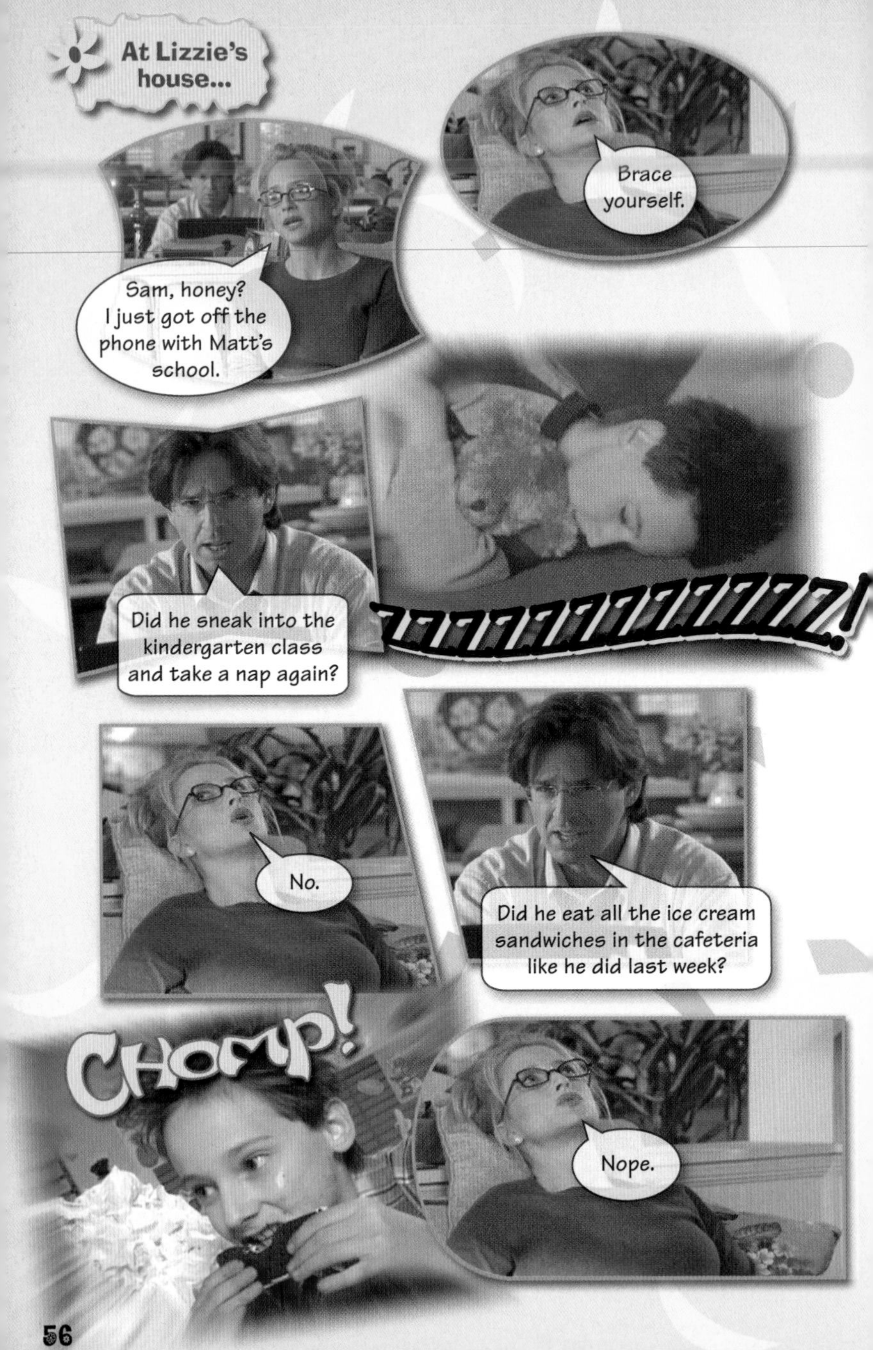
At Lizzie's house...
Sam, honey? I just got off the phone with Matt's school.
Brace yourself.
Did he sneak into the kindergarten class and take a nap again?
ZZZZZZZZZZZZZZZZ!
No.
Did he eat all the ice cream sandwiches in the cafeteria like he did last week?
CHOMP!
Nope.

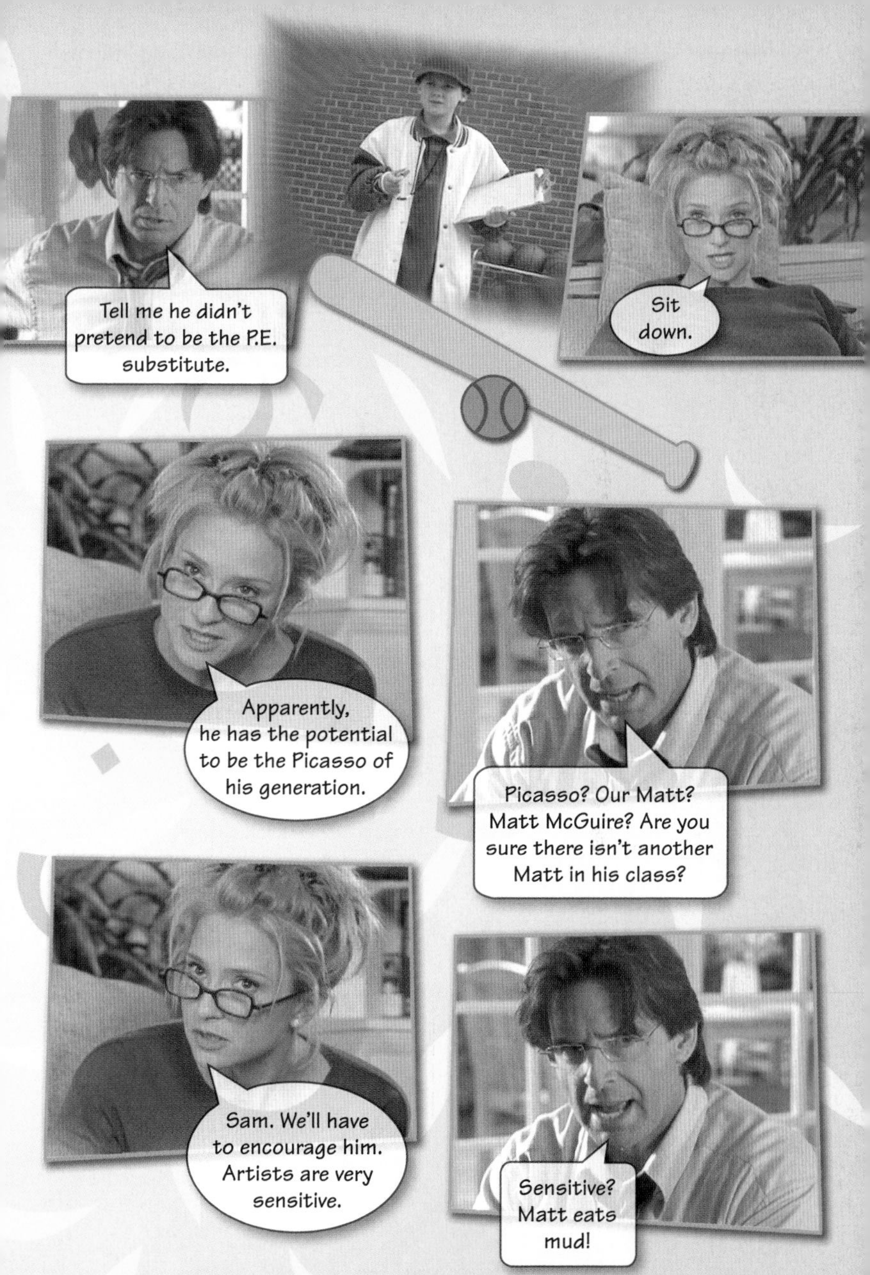
Tell me he didn't pretend to be the P.E. substitute.
Sit down.
Apparently, he has the potential to be the Picasso of his generation.
Picasso? Our Matt? Matt McGuire? Are you sure there isn't another Matt in his class?
Sam. We'll have to encourage him. Artists are very sensitive.
Sensitive? Matt eats mud!

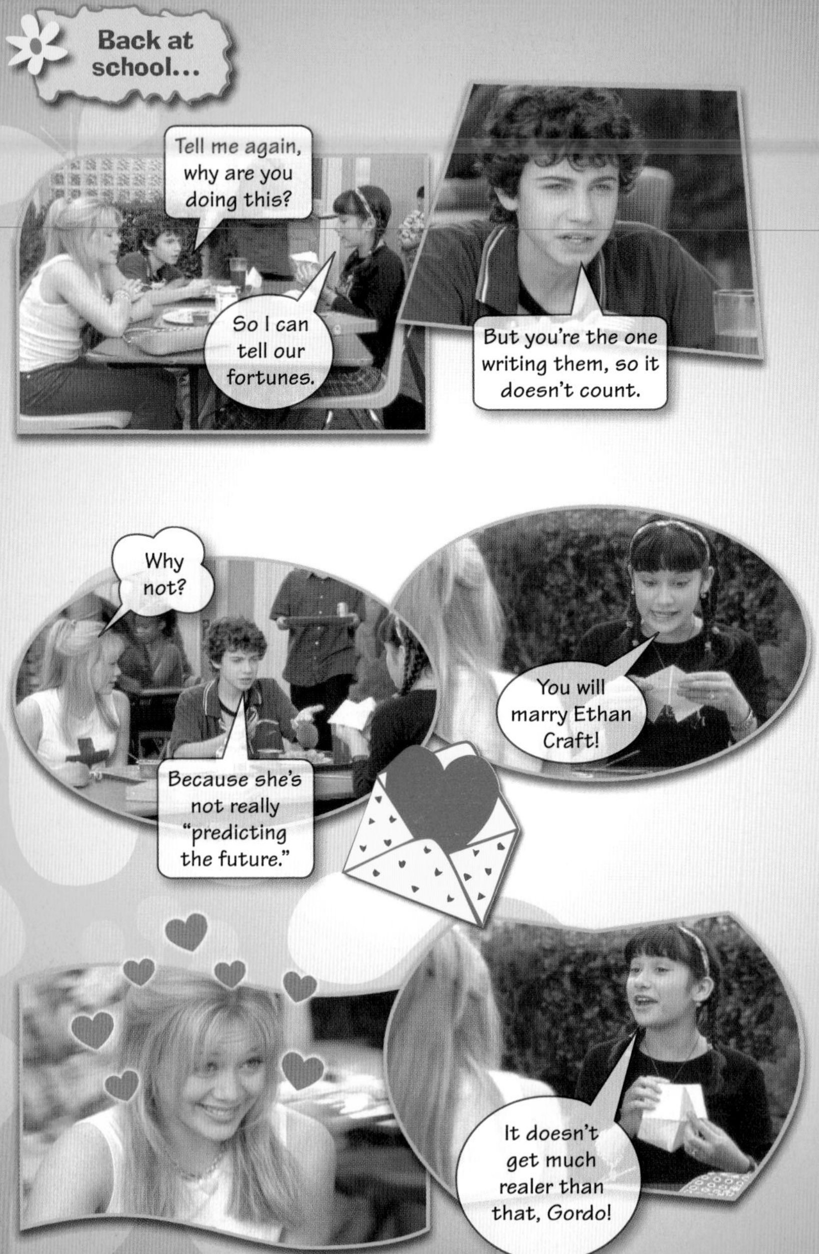
Back at school...
Tell me again, why are you doing this?
So I can tell our fortunes.
But you're the one writing them, so it doesn't count.
Why not?
Because she's not really "predicting the future."
You will marry Ethan Craft!
It doesn't get much realer than that, Gordo!

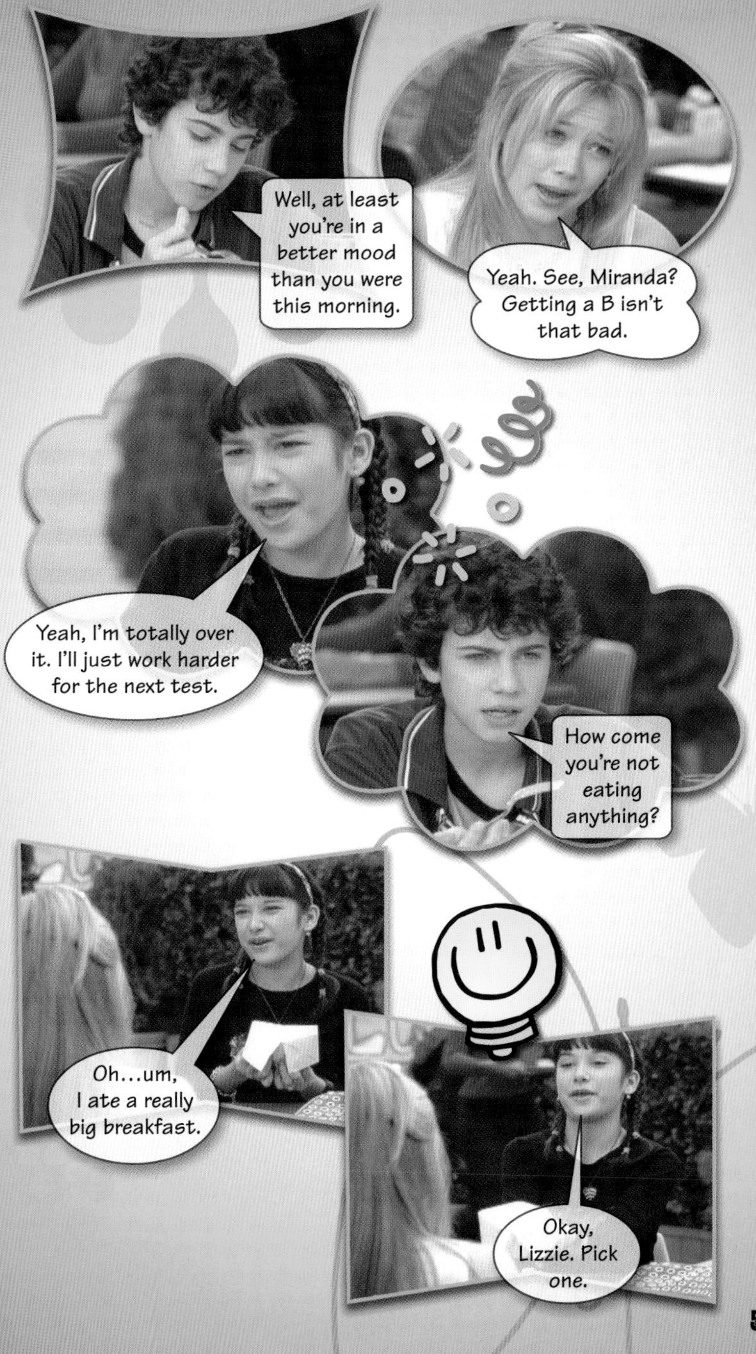
Well, at least you're in a better mood than you were this morning.
Yeah. See, Miranda? Getting a B isn't that bad.
Yeah, I'm totally over it. I'll just work harder for the next test.
How come you're not eating anything?
Oh...um, I ate a really big breakfast.
Okay, Lizzie. Pick one.

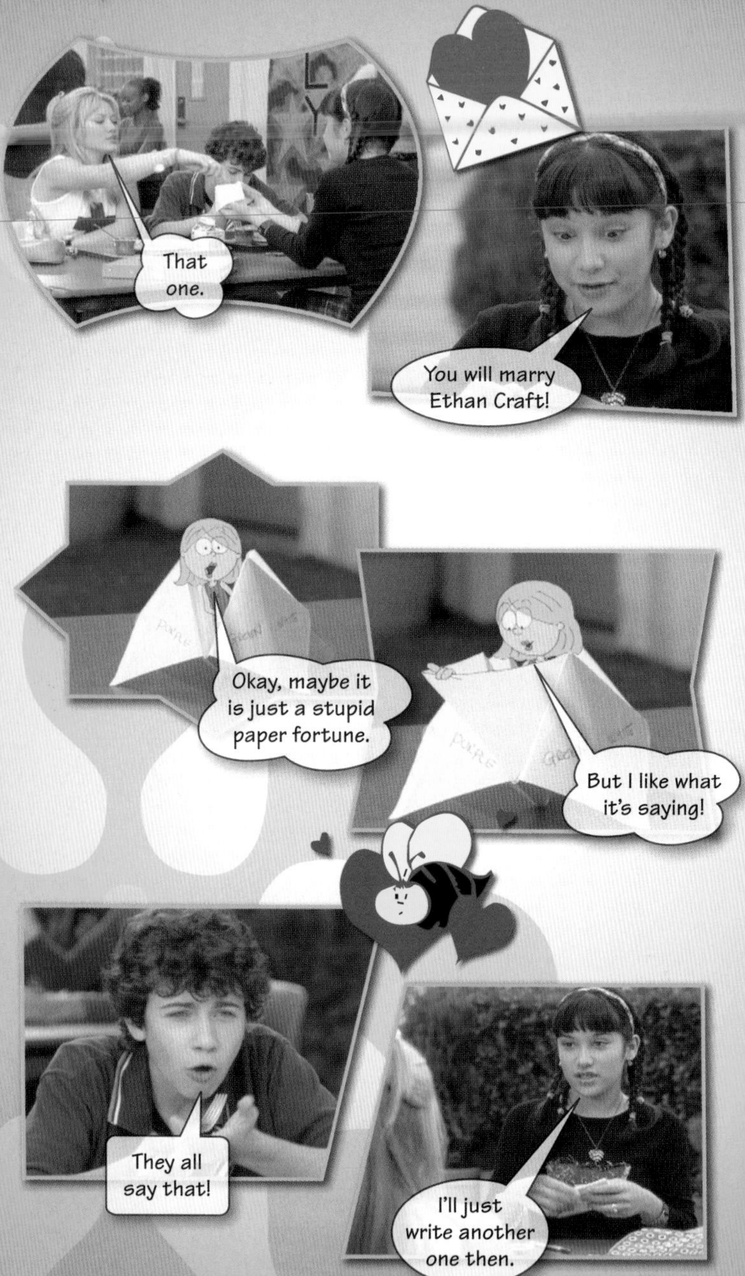
That one.
You will marry Ethan Craft!
Okay, maybe it is just a stupid paper fortune.
But I like what it's saying!
They all say that!
I'll just write another one then.

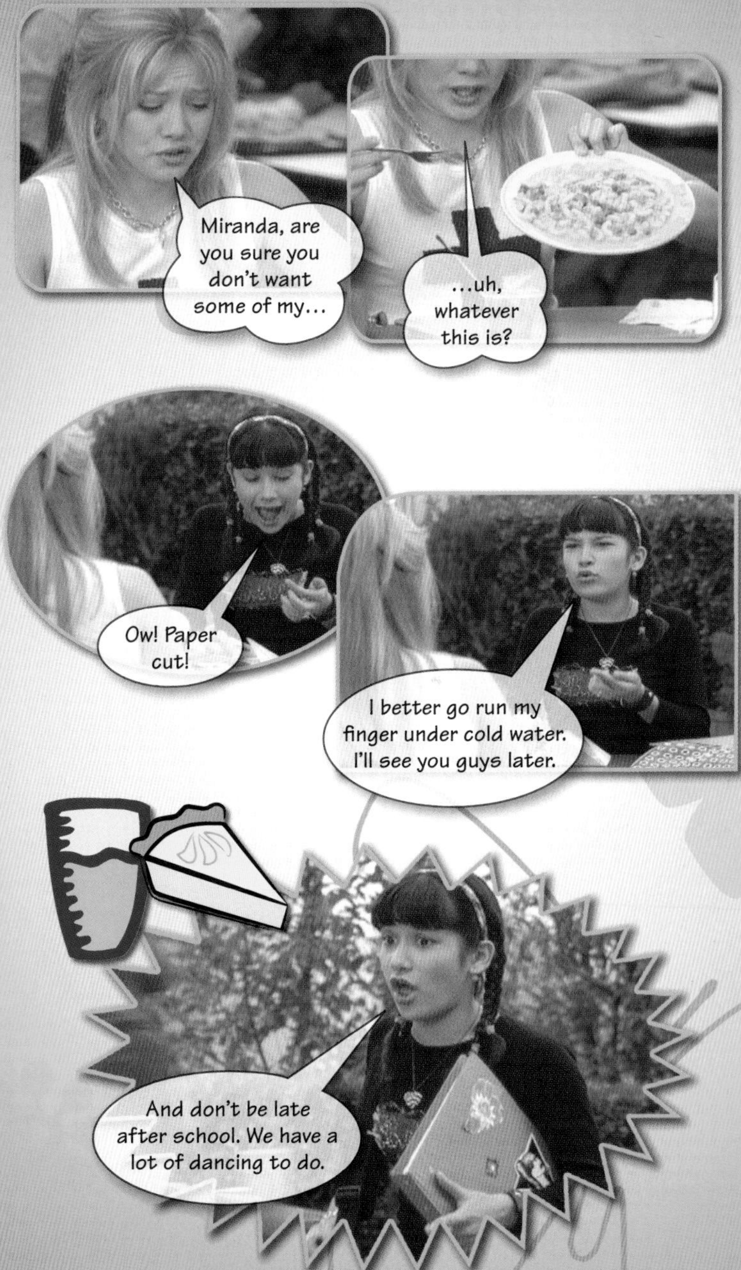
Miranda, are you sure you don't want some of my...
...uh, whatever this is?
Ow! Paper cut!
I better go run my finger under cold water. I'll see you guys later.
And don't be late after school. We have a lot of dancing to do.

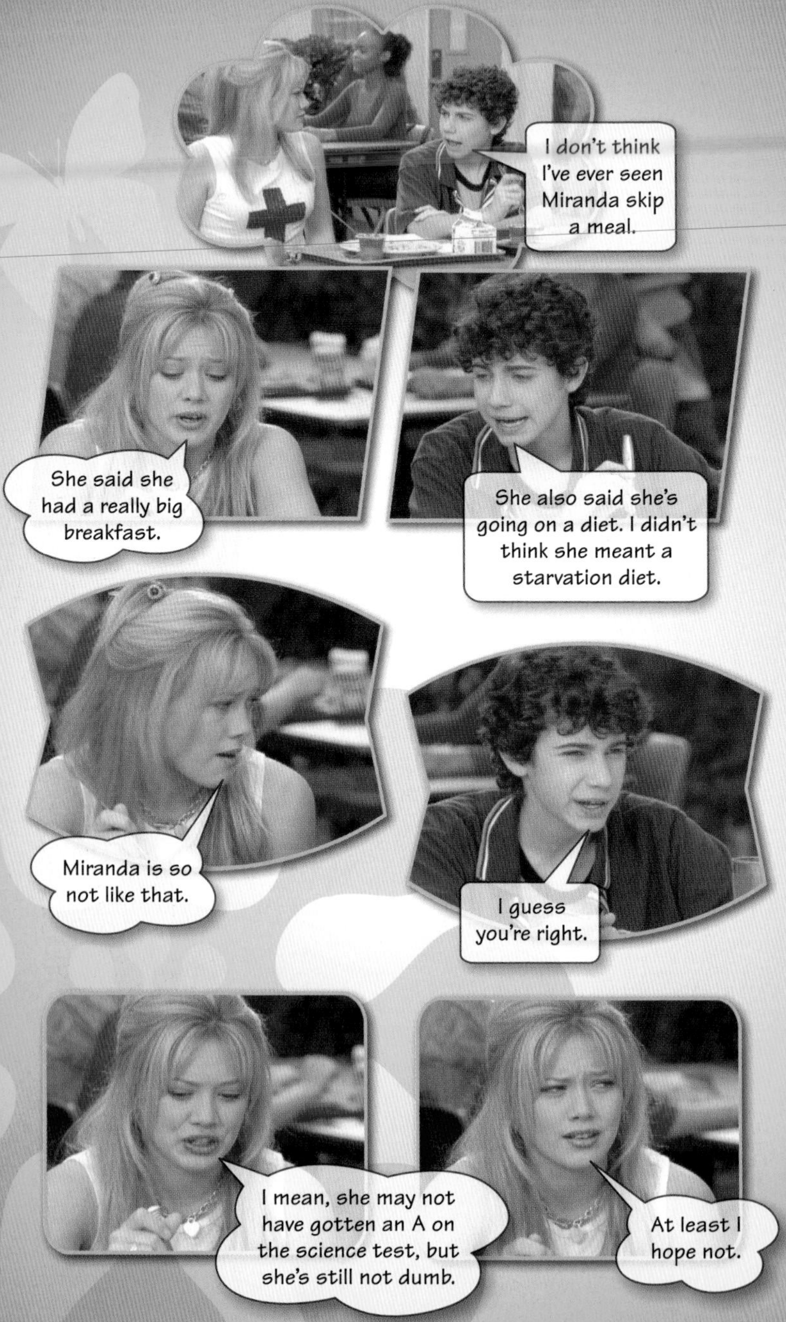
I don't think I've ever seen Miranda skip a meal.
She said she had a really big breakfast.
She also said she's going on a diet. I didn't think she meant a starvation diet.
Miranda is so not like that.
I guess you're right.
I mean, she may not have gotten an A on the science test, but she's still not dumb.
At least I hope not.

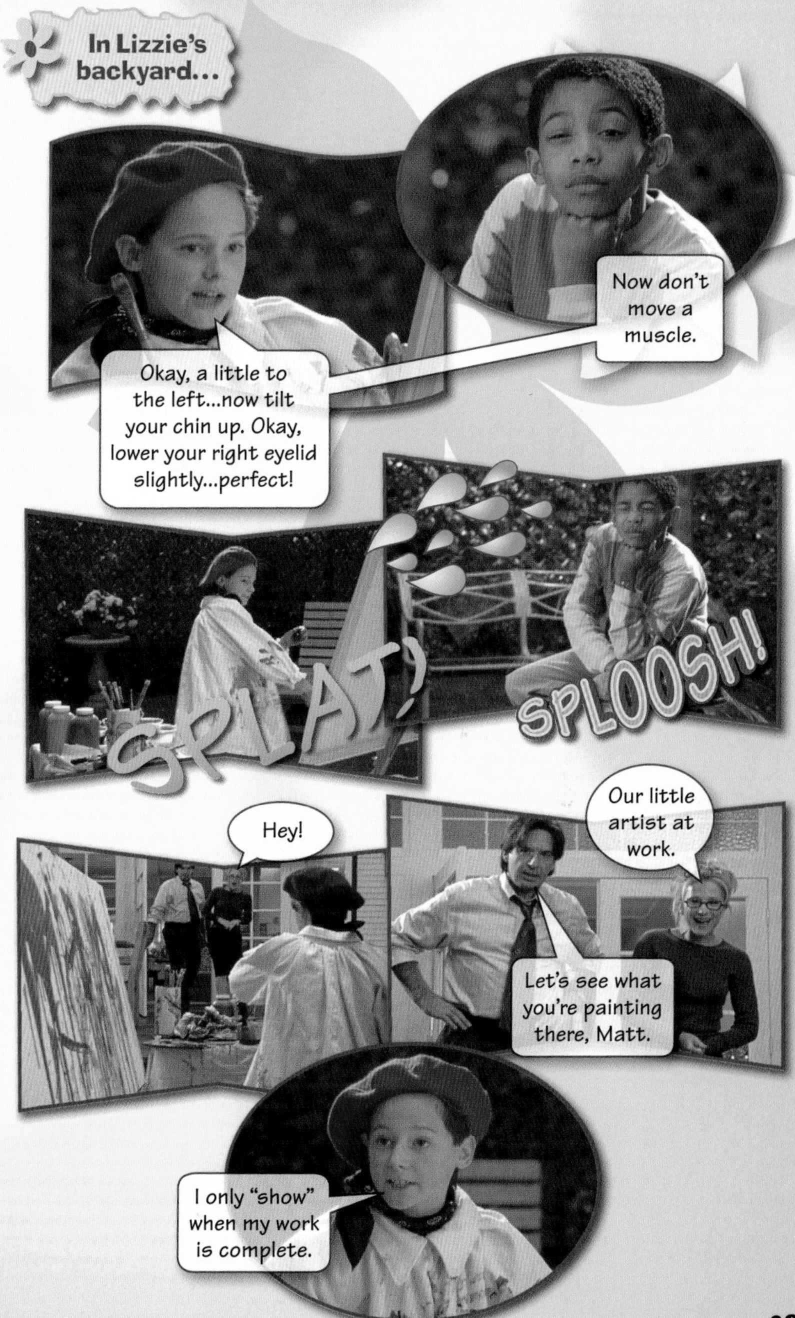
In Lizzie's backyard...
Okay, a little to the left...now tilt your chin up. Okay, lower your right eyelid slightly...perfect!
Now don't move a muscle.
SPLAT!
SPLOOSH!
Hey!
Our little artist at work.
Let's see what you're painting there, Matt.
I only "show" when my work is complete.

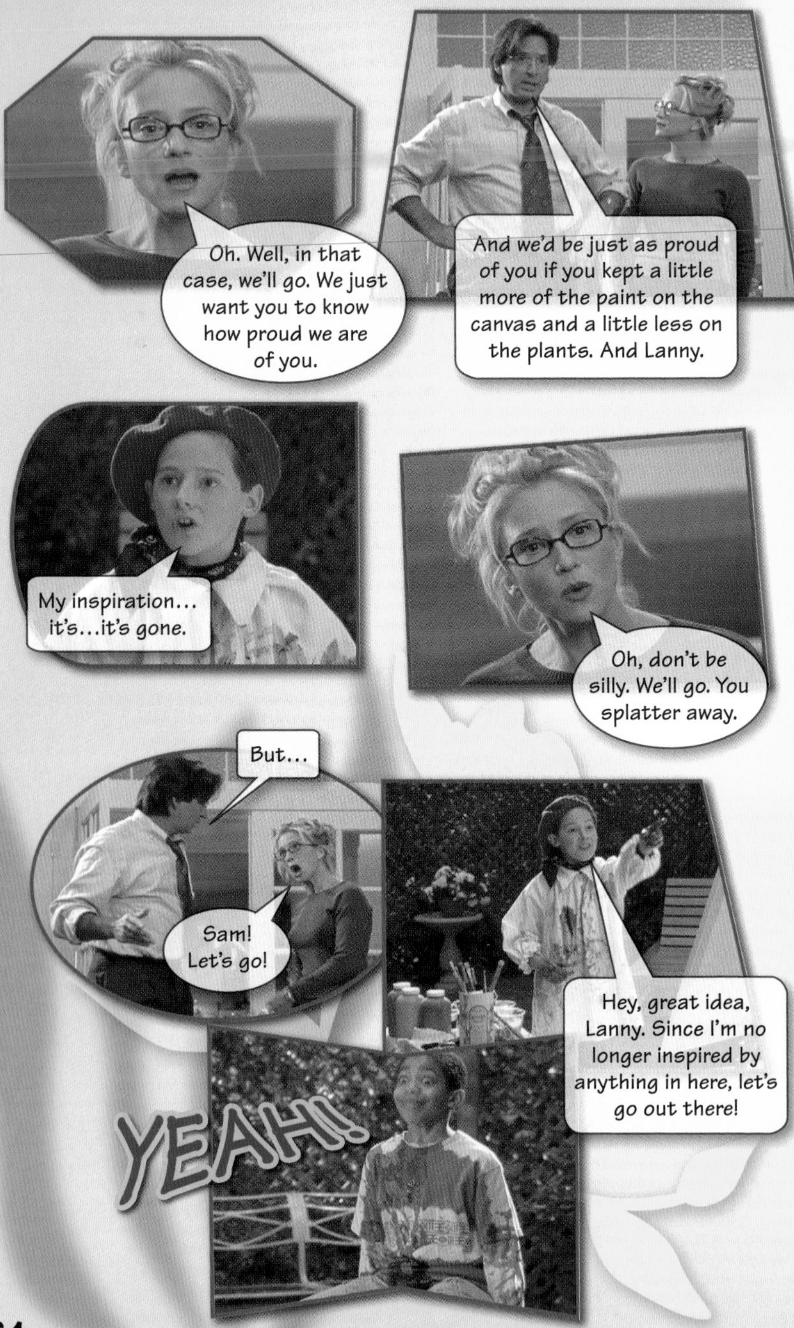
Oh. Well, in that case, we'll go. We just want you to know how proud we are of you.
And we'd be just as proud of you if you kept a little more of the paint on the canvas and a little less on the plants. And Lanny.
My inspiration… it's…it's gone.
Oh, don't be silly. We'll go. You splatter away.
But…
Sam! Let's go!
Hey, great idea, Lanny. Since I'm no longer inspired by anything in here, let's go out there!
YEAH!

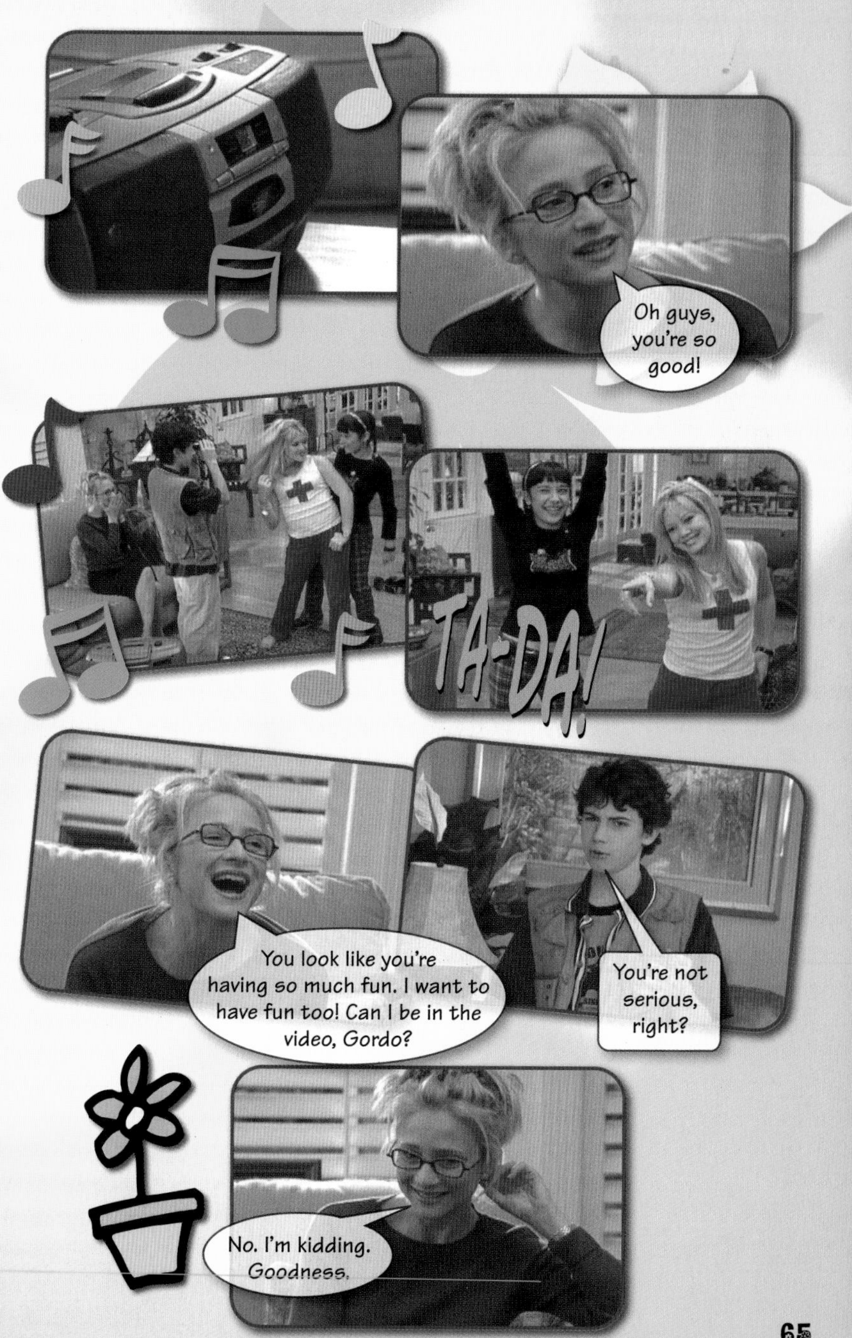
Oh guys, you're so good!
TA-DA!
You look like you're having so much fun. I want to have fun too! Can I be in the video, Gordo?
You're not serious, right?
No. I'm kidding. Goodness.

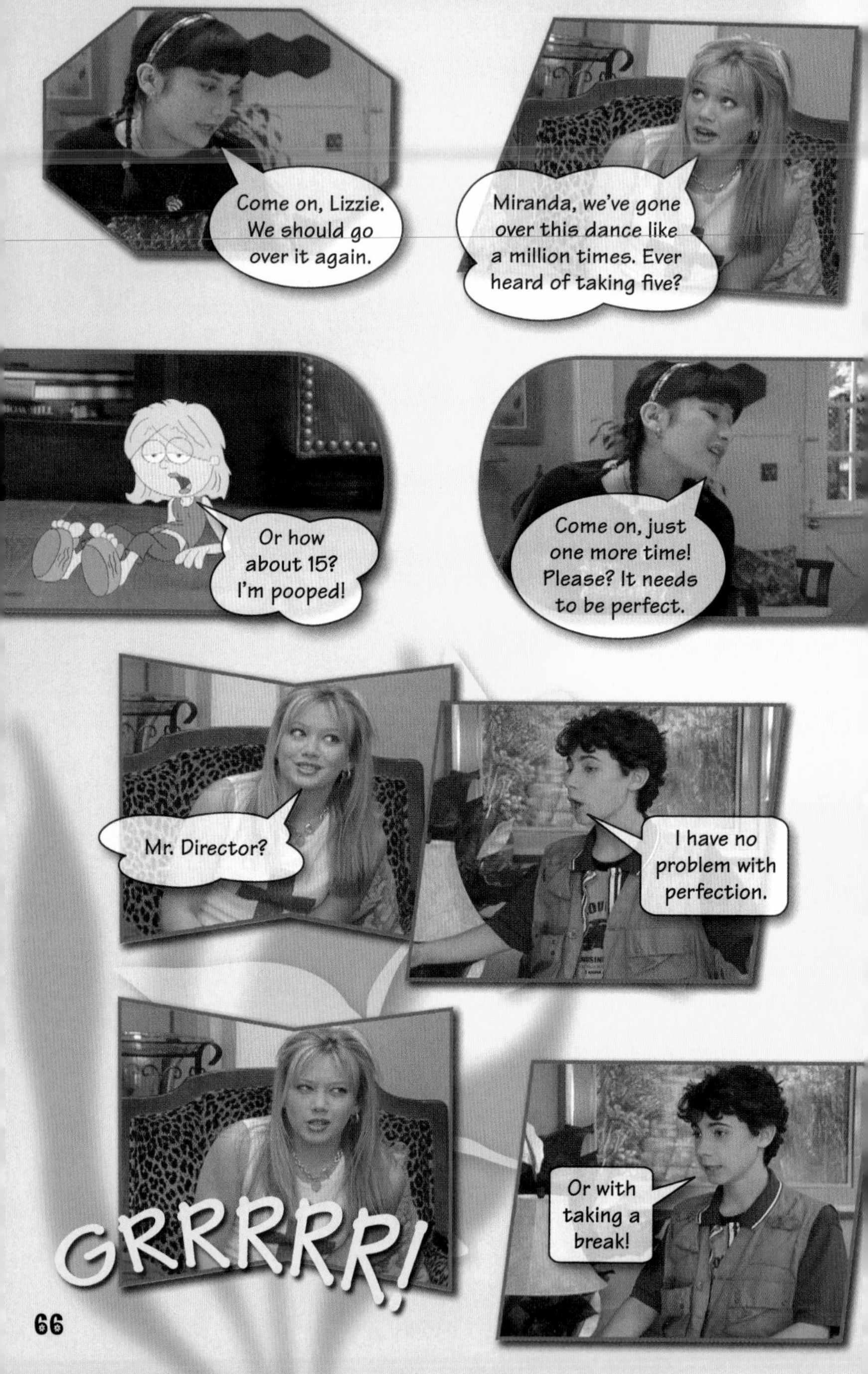
Come on, Lizzie. We should go over it again.
Miranda, we've gone over this dance like a million times. Ever heard of taking five?
Or how about 15? I'm pooped!
Come on, just one more time! Please? It needs to be perfect.
Mr. Director?
I have no problem with perfection.
GRRRRR!
Or with taking a break!

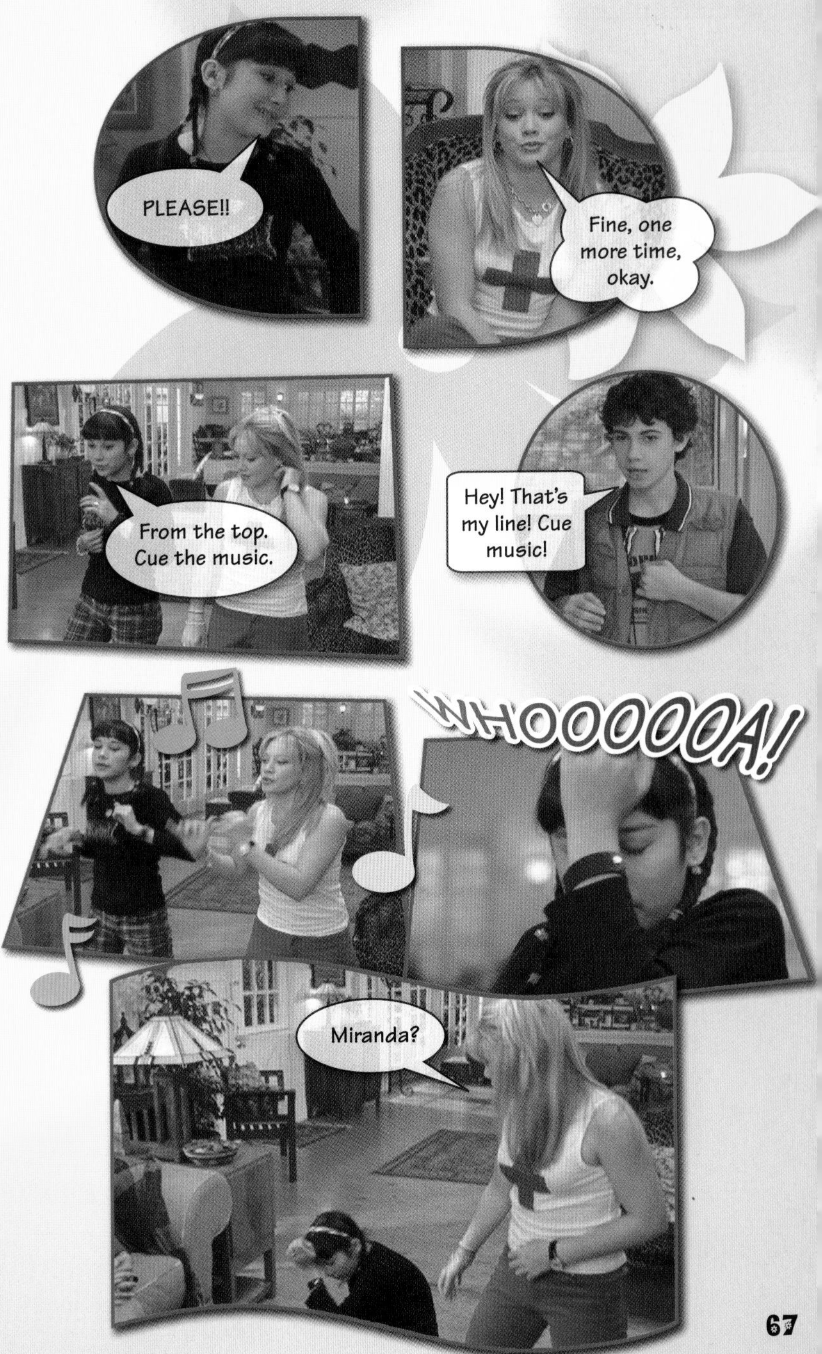
PLEASE!!
Fine, one more time, okay.
From the top. Cue the music.
Hey! That's my line! Cue music!
WHOOOOOA!
Miranda?

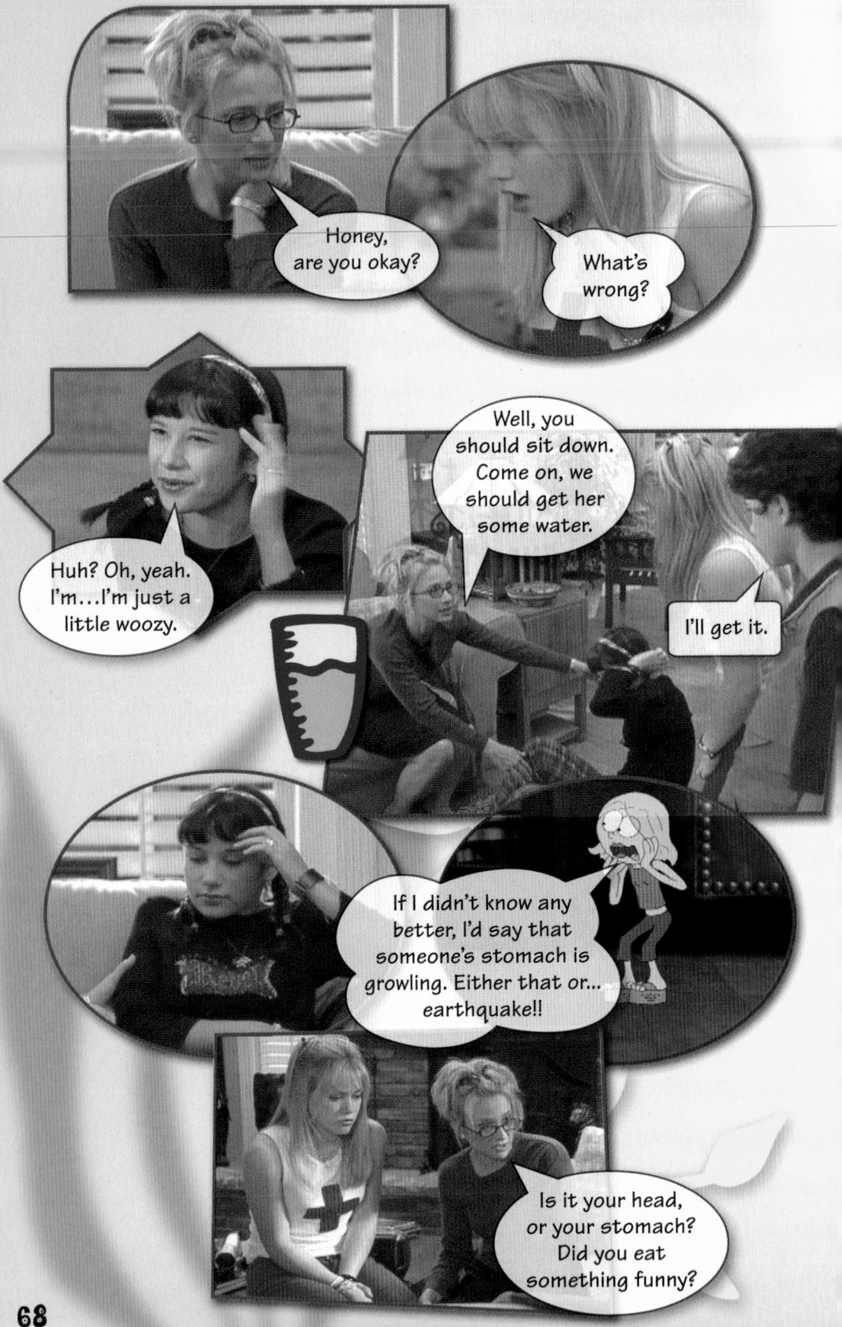

Honey, are you okay?
What's wrong?
Huh? Oh, yeah. I'm…I'm just a little woozy.
Well, you should sit down. Come on, we should get her some water.
I'll get it.
If I didn't know any better, I'd say that someone's stomach is growling. Either that or… earthquake!!
Is it your head, or your stomach? Did you eat something funny?

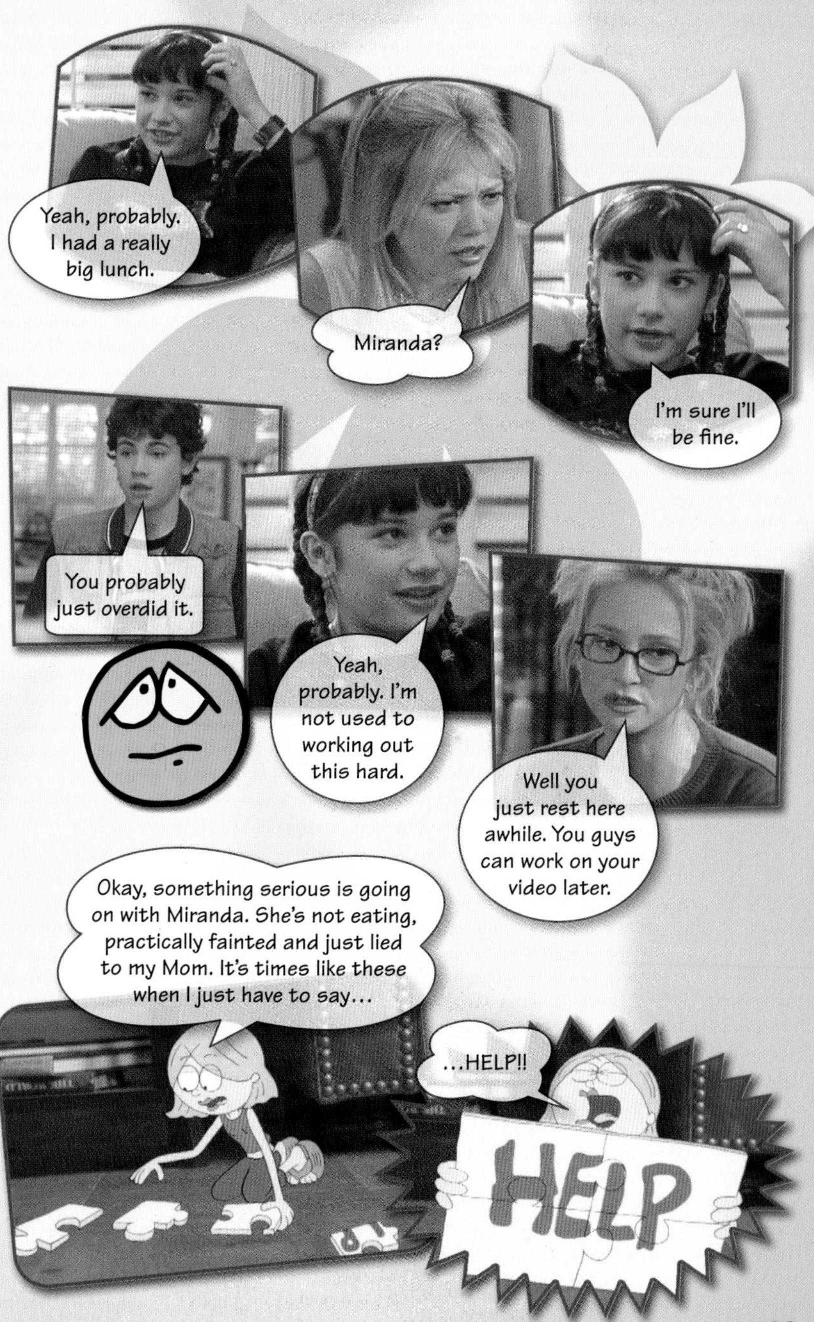

Yeah, probably. I had a really big lunch.
Miranda?
I'm sure I'll be fine.
You probably just overdid it.
Yeah, probably. I'm not used to working out this hard.
Well you just rest here awhile. You guys can work on your video later.
Okay, something serious is going on with Miranda. She's not eating, practically fainted and just lied to my Mom. It's times like these when I just have to say...
...HELP!!
HELP

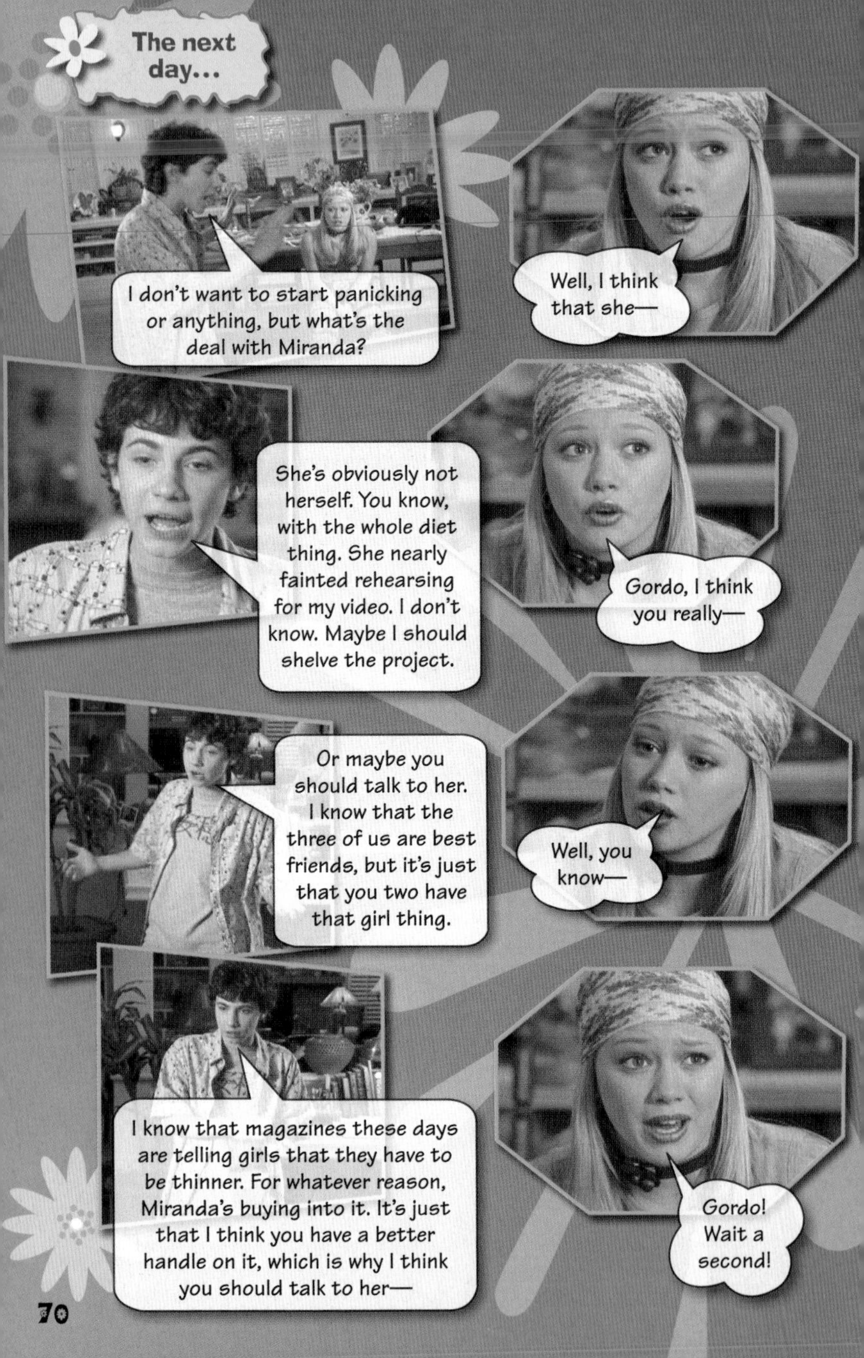
The next day...
I don't want to start panicking or anything, but what's the deal with Miranda?
Well, I think that she—
She's obviously not herself. You know, with the whole diet thing. She nearly fainted rehearsing for my video. I don't know. Maybe I should shelve the project.
Gordo, I think you really—
Or maybe you should talk to her. I know that the three of us are best friends, but it's just that you two have that girl thing.
Well, you know—
I know that magazines these days are telling girls that they have to be thinner. For whatever reason, Miranda's buying into it. It's just that I think you have a better handle on it, which is why I think you should talk to her—
Gordo! Wait a second!

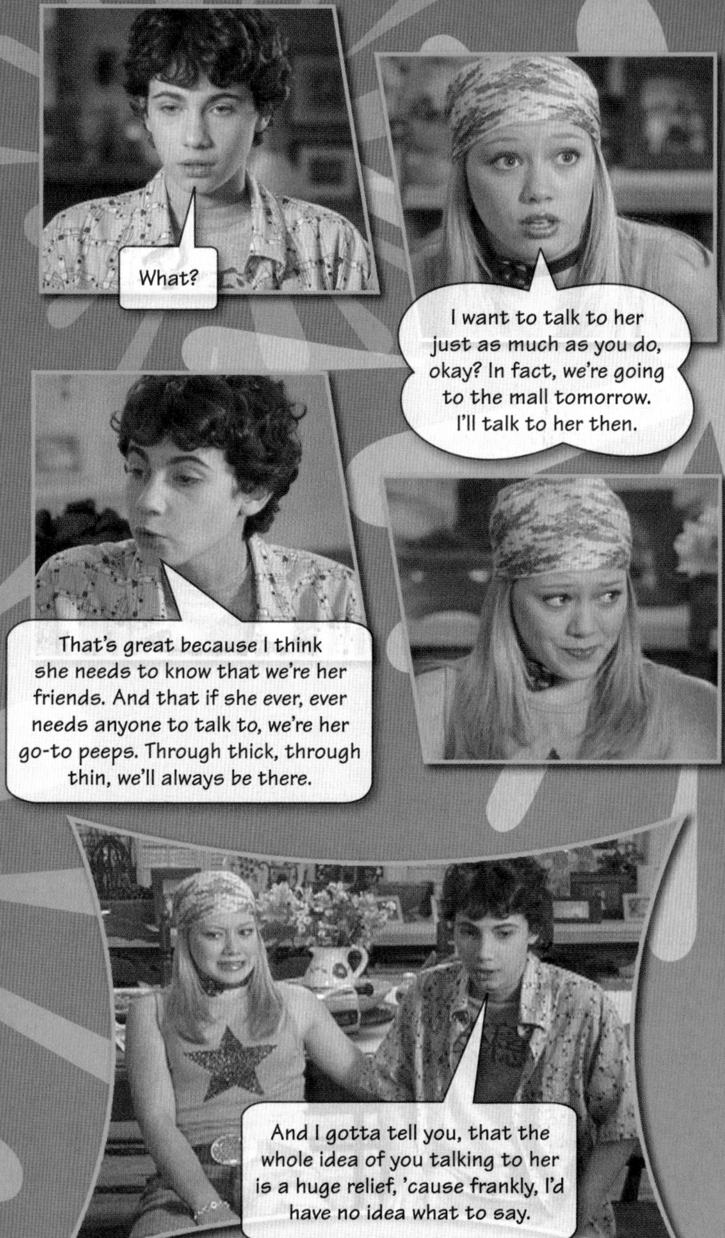
What?
I want to talk to her just as much as you do, okay? In fact, we're going to the mall tomorrow. I'll talk to her then.
That's great because I think she needs to know that we're her friends. And that if she ever, ever needs anyone to talk to, we're her go-to peeps. Through thick, through thin, we'll always be there.
And I gotta tell you, that the whole idea of you talking to her is a huge relief, 'cause frankly, I'd have no idea what to say.

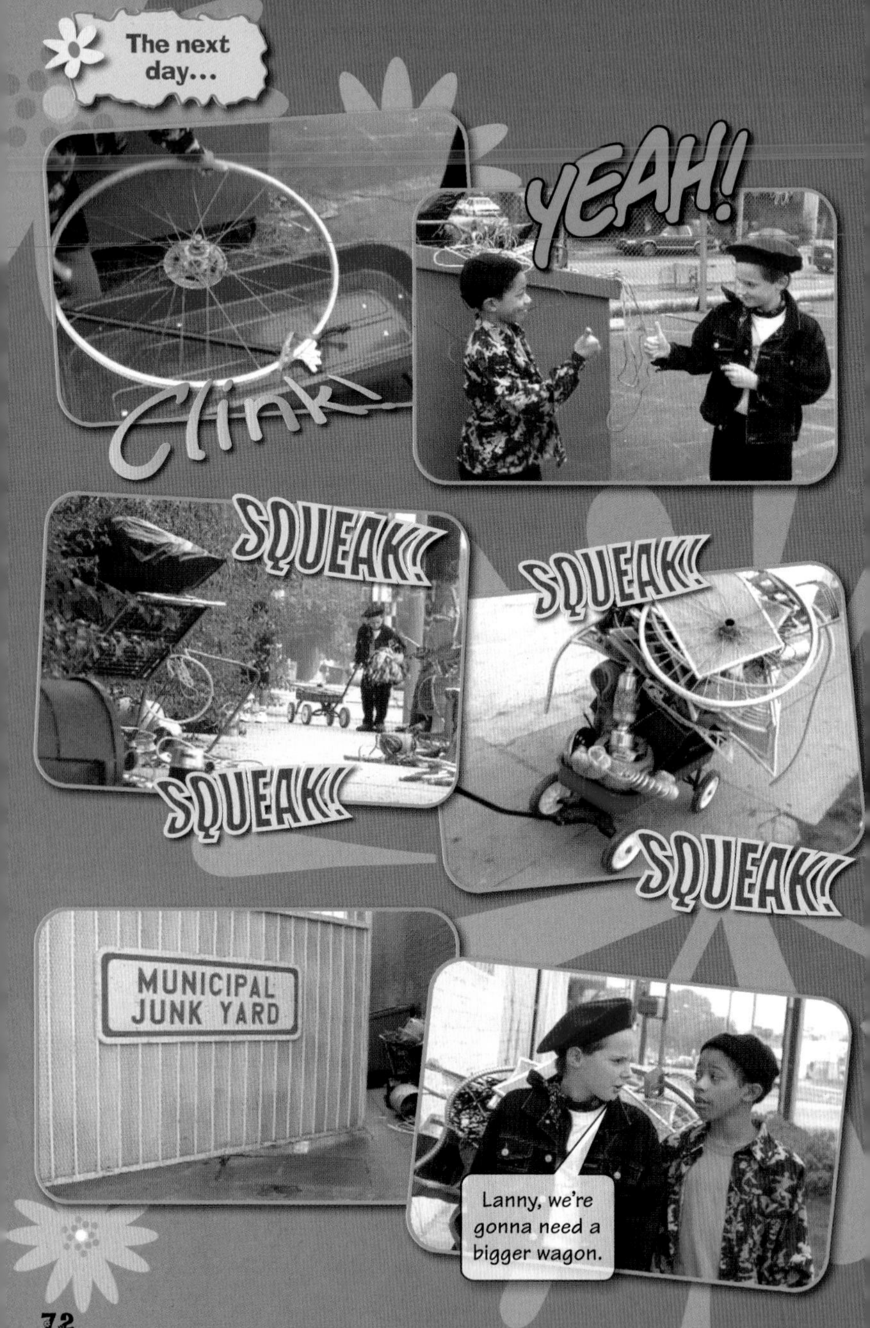
The next day...
Clink
YEAH!
SQUEAK!
SQUEAK!
SQUEAK!
SQUEAK!
MUNICIPAL JUNK YARD
Lanny, we're gonna need a bigger wagon.

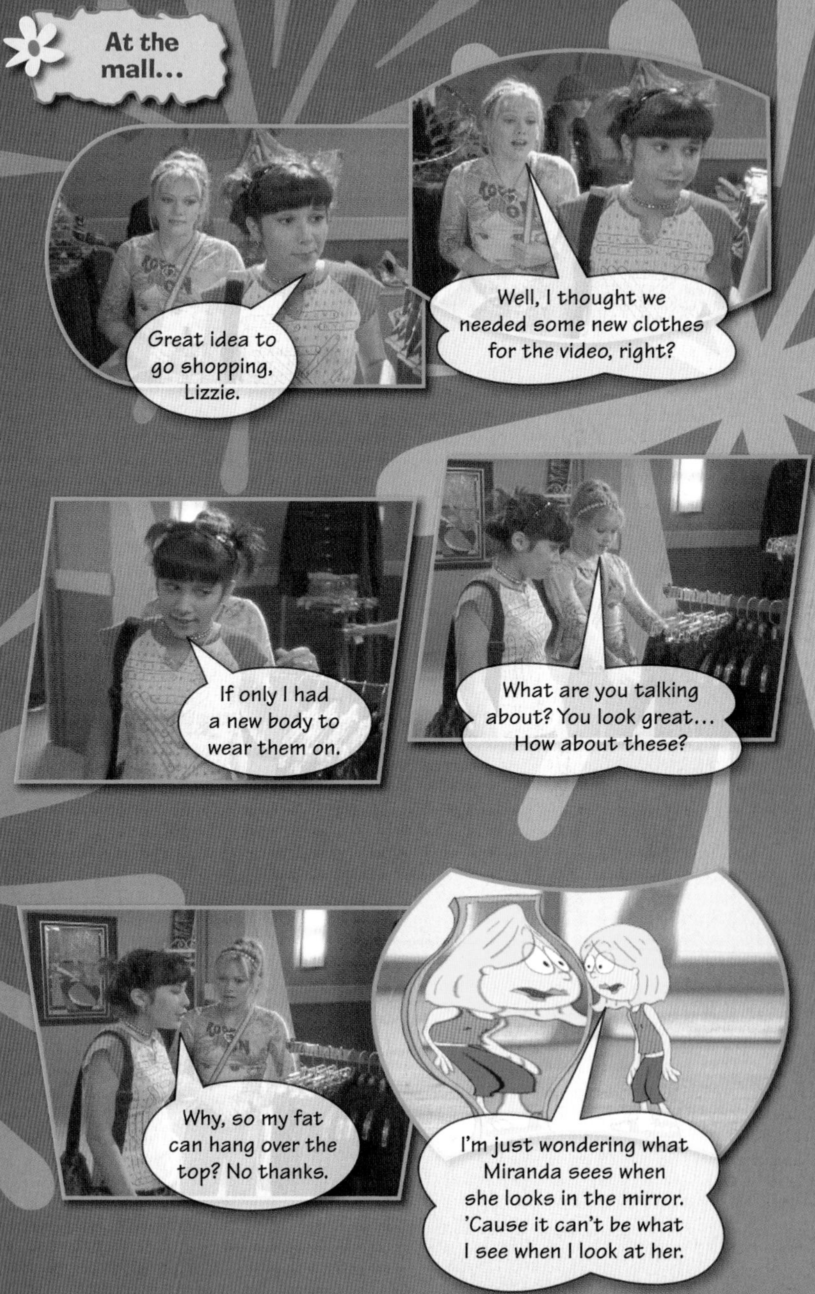
At the mall...
Great idea to go shopping, Lizzie.
Well, I thought we needed some new clothes for the video, right?
If only I had a new body to wear them on.
What are you talking about? You look great... How about these?
Why, so my fat can hang over the top? No thanks.
I'm just wondering what Miranda sees when she looks in the mirror. 'Cause it can't be what I see when I look at her.

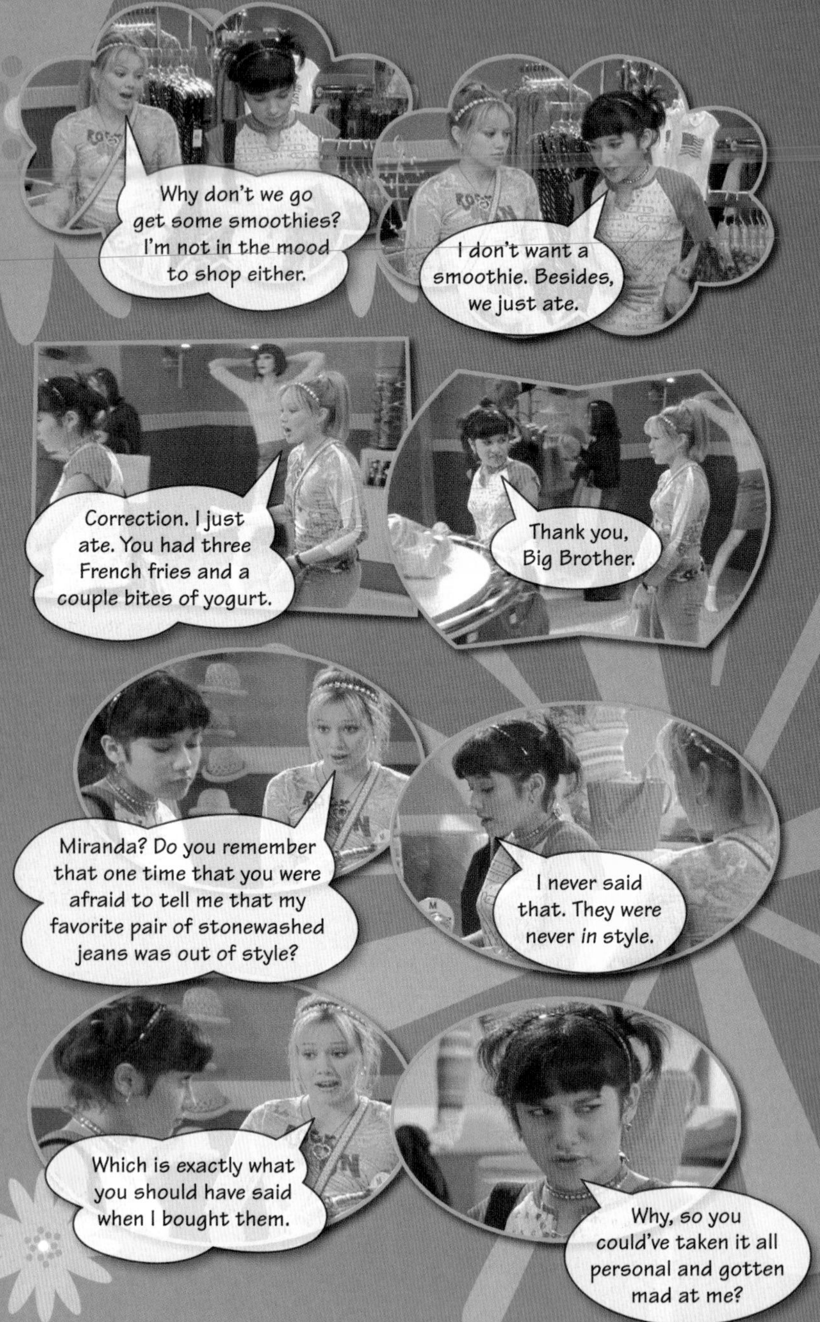
Why don't we go get some smoothies? I'm not in the mood to shop either.
I don't want a smoothie. Besides, we just ate.
Correction. I just ate. You had three French fries and a couple bites of yogurt.
Thank you, Big Brother.
Miranda? Do you remember that one time that you were afraid to tell me that my favorite pair of stonewashed jeans was out of style?
I never said that. They were never *in* style.
Which is exactly what you should have said when I bought them.
Why, so you could've taken it all personal and gotten mad at me?

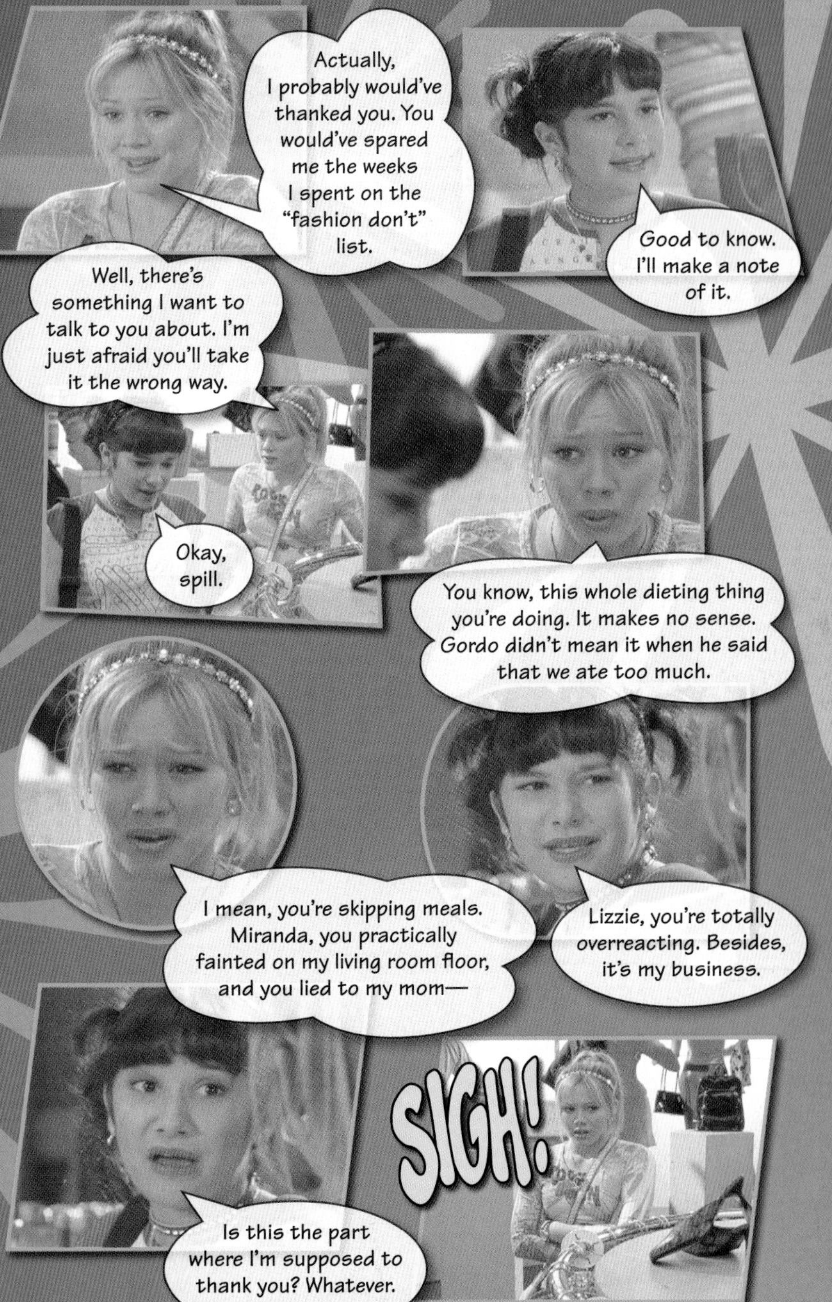
Actually, I probably would've thanked you. You would've spared me the weeks I spent on the "fashion don't" list.
Good to know. I'll make a note of it.
Well, there's something I want to talk to you about. I'm just afraid you'll take it the wrong way.
Okay, spill.
You know, this whole dieting thing you're doing. It makes no sense. Gordo didn't mean it when he said that we ate too much.
I mean, you're skipping meals. Miranda, you practically fainted on my living room floor, and you lied to my mom—
Lizzie, you're totally overreacting. Besides, it's my business.
Is this the part where I'm supposed to thank you? Whatever. I'm outie.
SIGH!

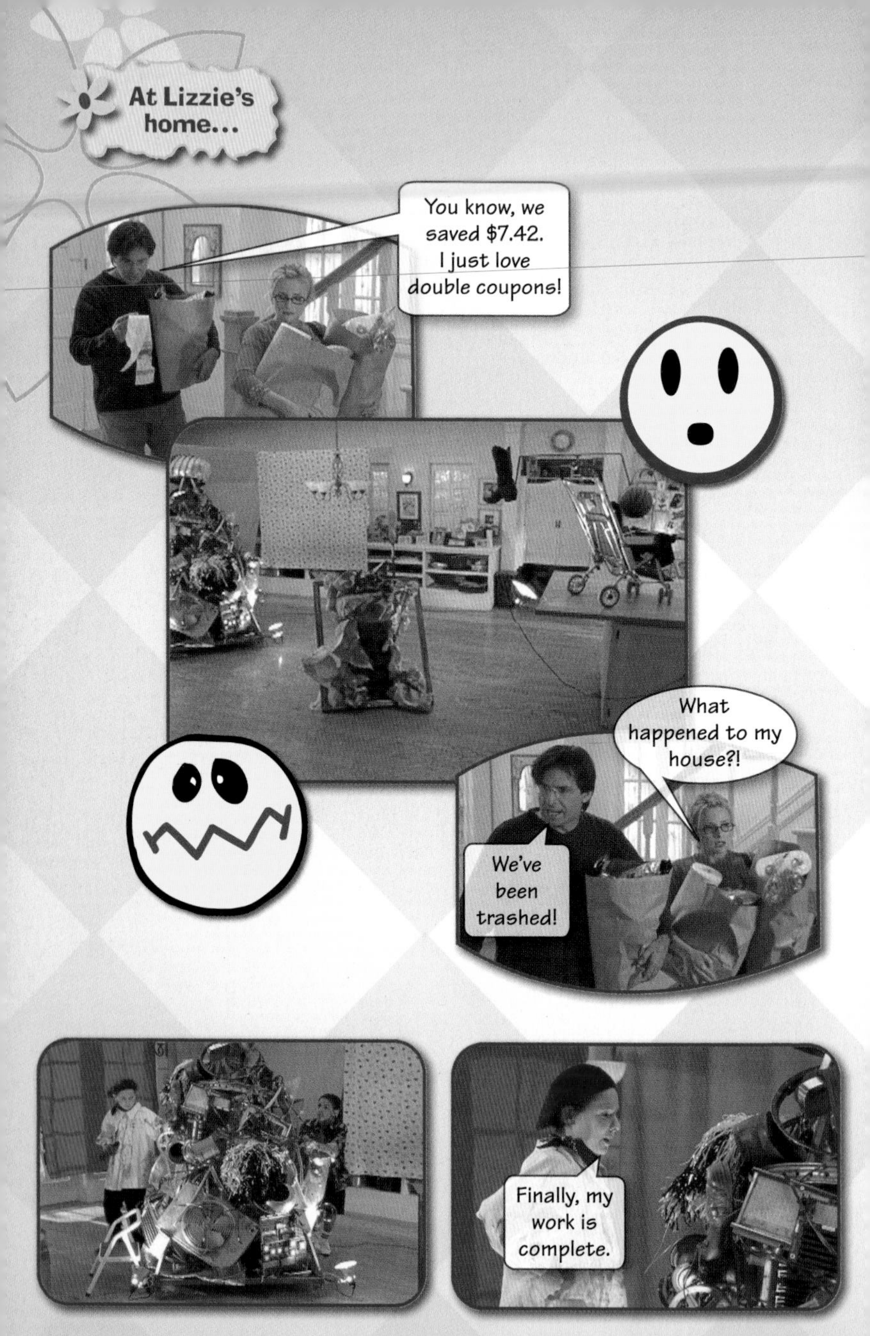
At Lizzie's home...
You know, we saved $7.42. I just love double coupons!
What happened to my house?!
We've been trashed!
Finally, my work is complete.

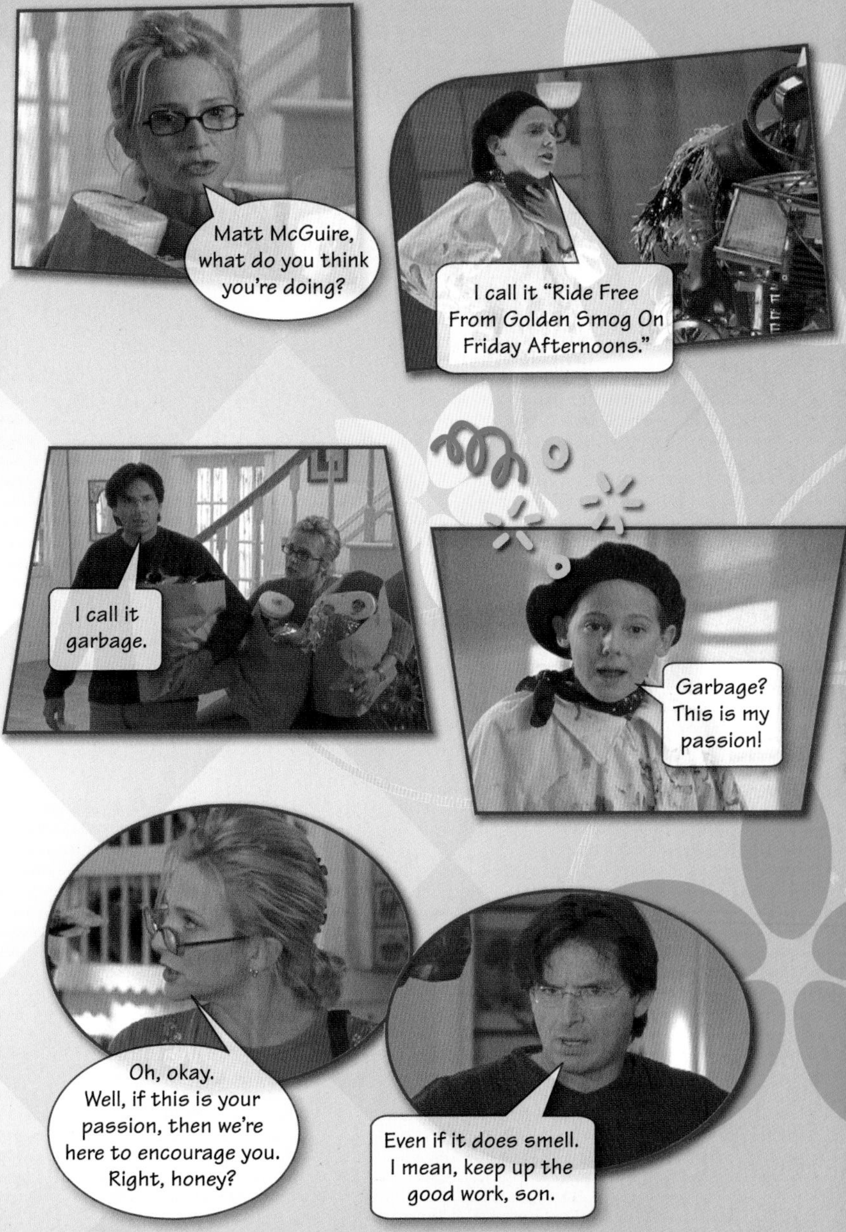
Matt McGuire, what do you think you're doing?
I call it "Ride Free From Golden Smog On Friday Afternoons."
I call it garbage.
Garbage? This is my passion!
Oh, okay. Well, if this is your passion, then we're here to encourage you. Right, honey?
Even if it does smell. I mean, keep up the good work, son.

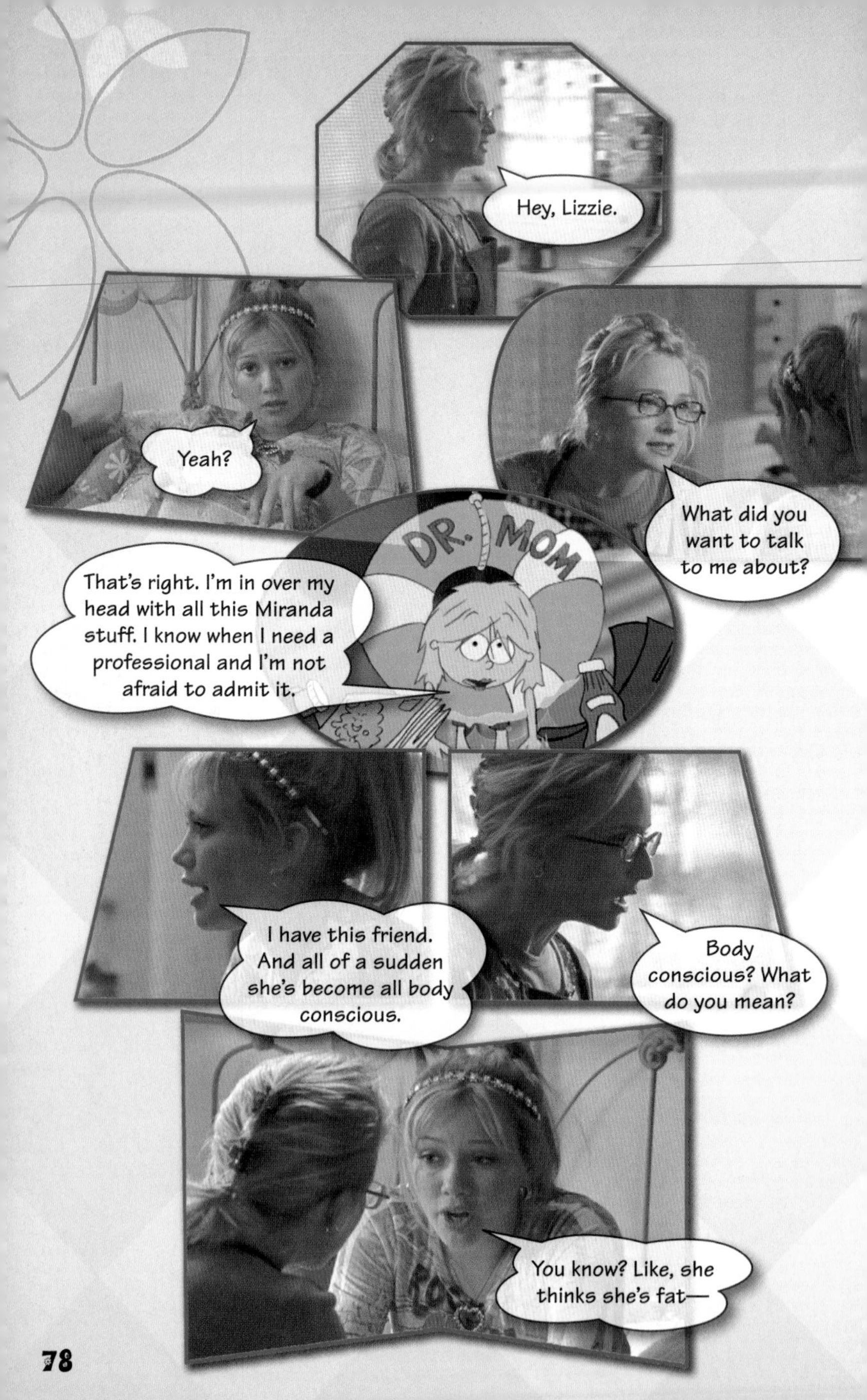
Hey, Lizzie.
Yeah?
What did you want to talk to me about?
DR. MOM
That's right. I'm in over my head with all this Miranda stuff. I know when I need a professional and I'm not afraid to admit it.
I have this friend. And all of a sudden she's become all body conscious.
Body conscious? What do you mean?
You know? Like, she thinks she's fat—

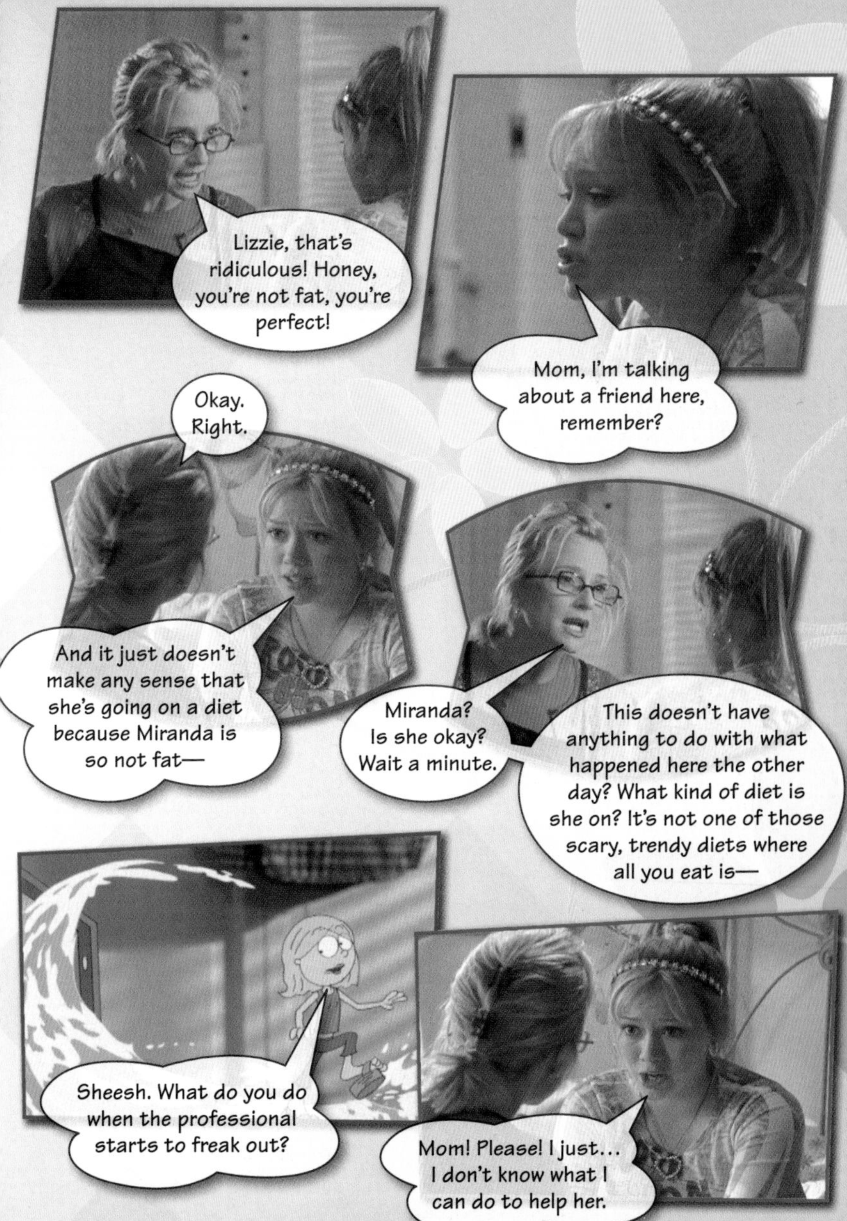
Lizzie, that's ridiculous! Honey, you're not fat, you're perfect!
Mom, I'm talking about a friend here, remember?
Okay. Right.
And it just doesn't make any sense that she's going on a diet because Miranda is so not fat—
Miranda? Is she okay? Wait a minute.
This doesn't have anything to do with what happened here the other day? What kind of diet is she on? It's not one of those scary, trendy diets where all you eat is—
Sheesh. What do you do when the professional starts to freak out?
Mom! Please! I just... I don't know what I can do to help her.

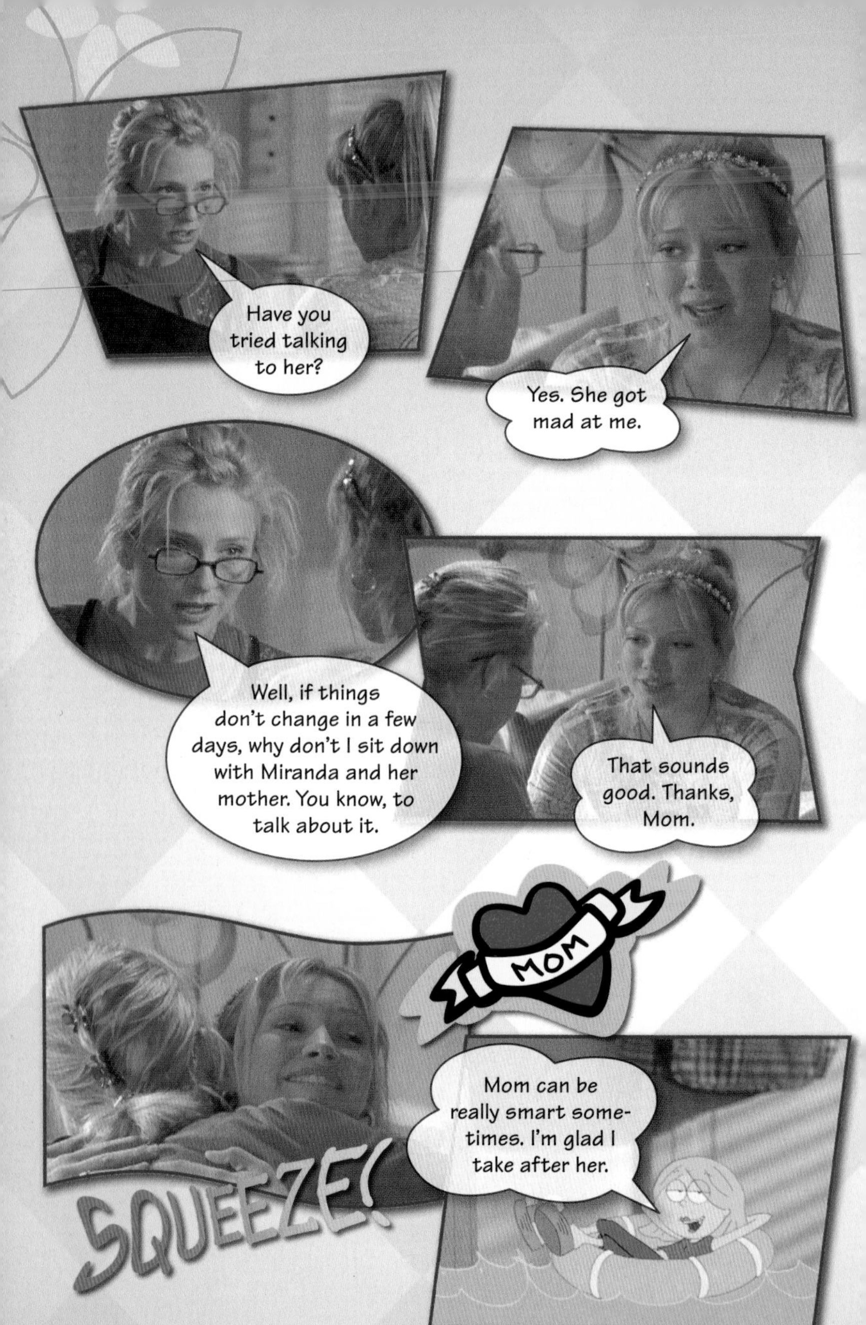
Have you tried talking to her?
Yes. She got mad at me.
Well, if things don't change in a few days, why don't I sit down with Miranda and her mother. You know, to talk about it.
That sounds good. Thanks, Mom.
MOM
SQUEEZE!
Mom can be really smart sometimes. I'm glad I take after her.

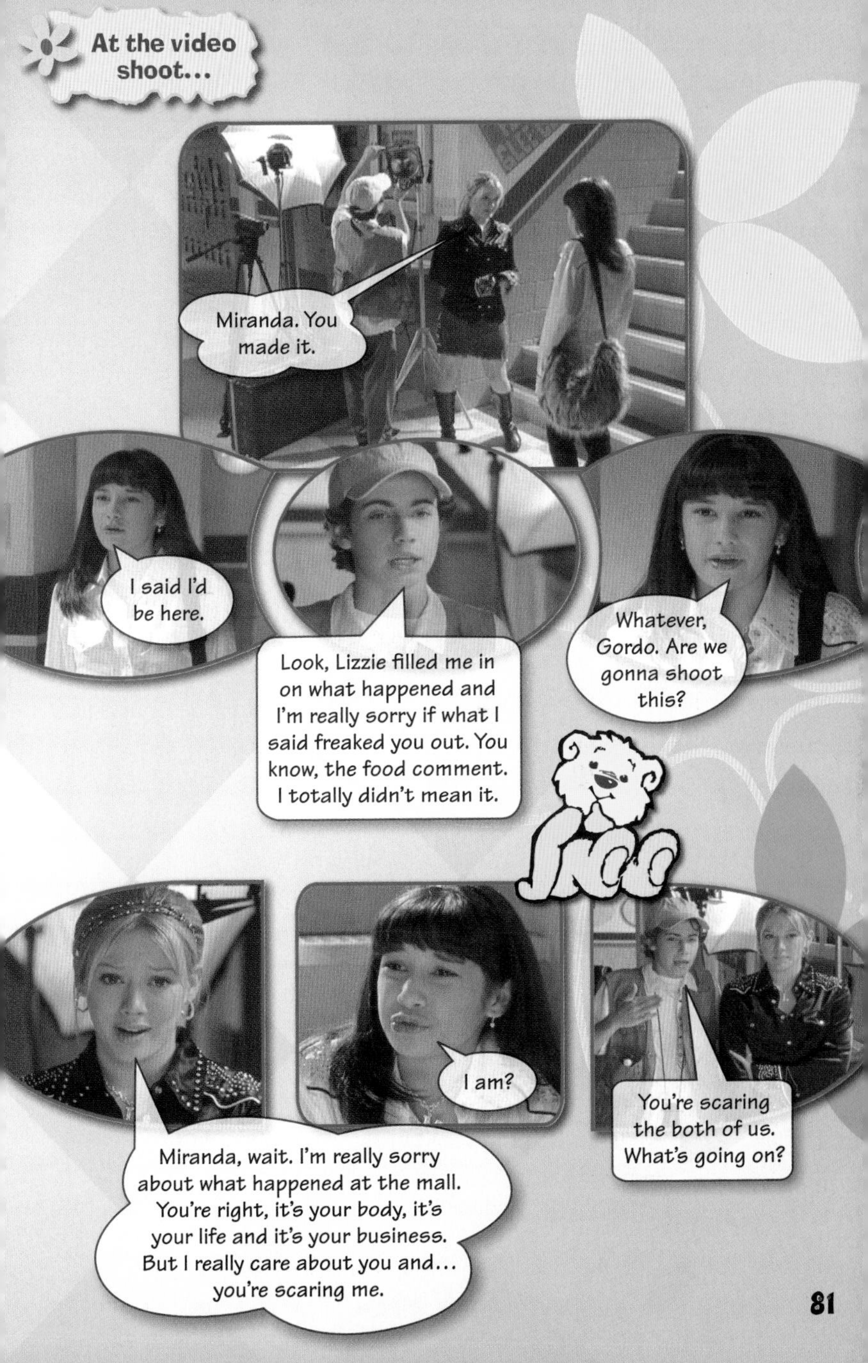
At the video shoot...
Miranda. You made it.
I said I'd be here.
Look, Lizzie filled me in on what happened and I'm really sorry if what I said freaked you out. You know, the food comment. I totally didn't mean it.
Whatever, Gordo. Are we gonna shoot this?
Miranda, wait. I'm really sorry about what happened at the mall. You're right, it's your body, it's your life and it's your business. But I really care about you and... you're scaring me.
I am?
You're scaring the both of us. What's going on?

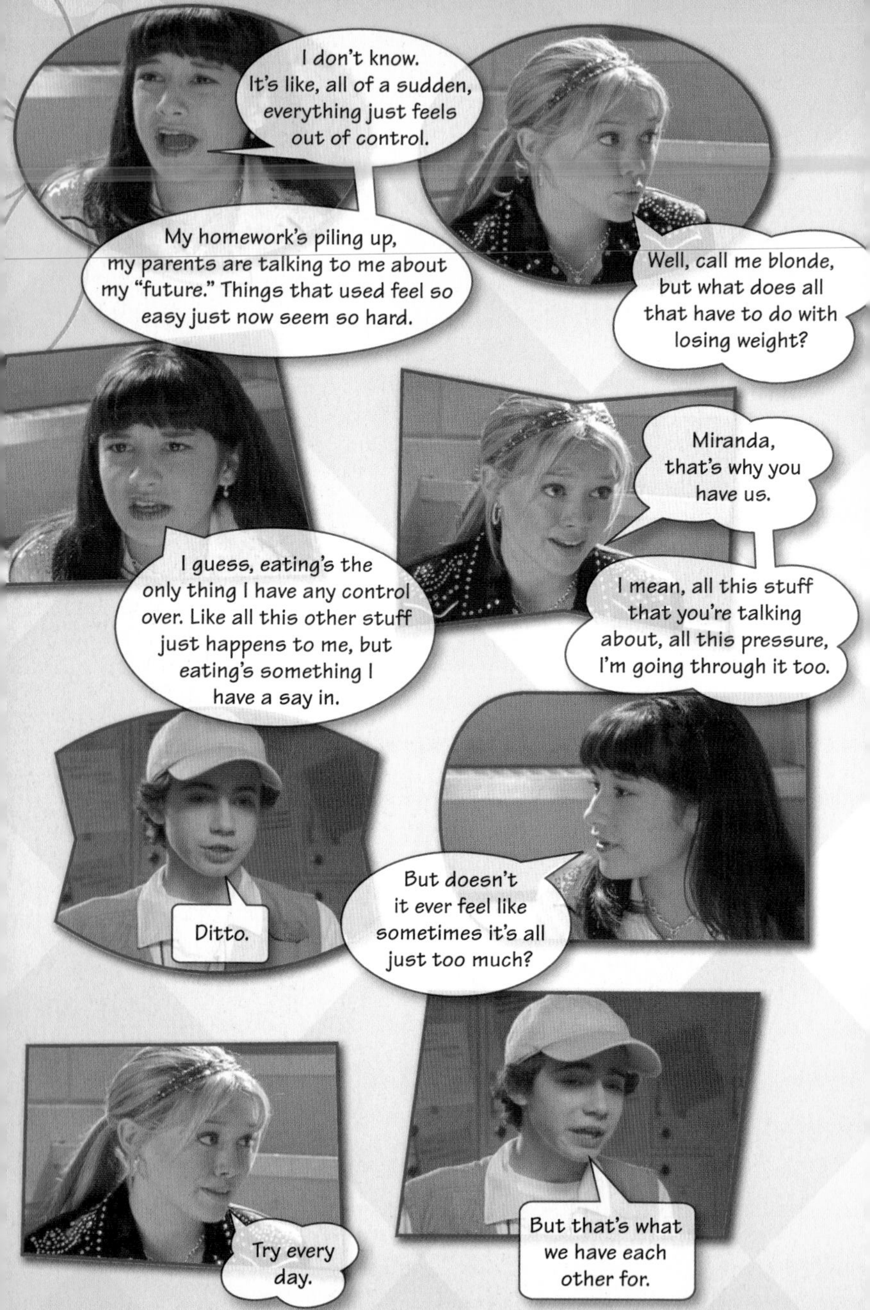
I don't know. It's like, all of a sudden, everything just feels out of control.
My homework's piling up, my parents are talking to me about my "future." Things that used feel so easy just now seem so hard.
Well, call me blonde, but what does all that have to do with losing weight?
I guess, eating's the only thing I have any control over. Like all this other stuff just happens to me, but eating's something I have a say in.
Miranda, that's why you have us.
I mean, all this stuff that you're talking about, all this pressure, I'm going through it too.
Ditto.
But doesn't it ever feel like sometimes it's all just too much?
Try every day.
But that's what we have each other for.

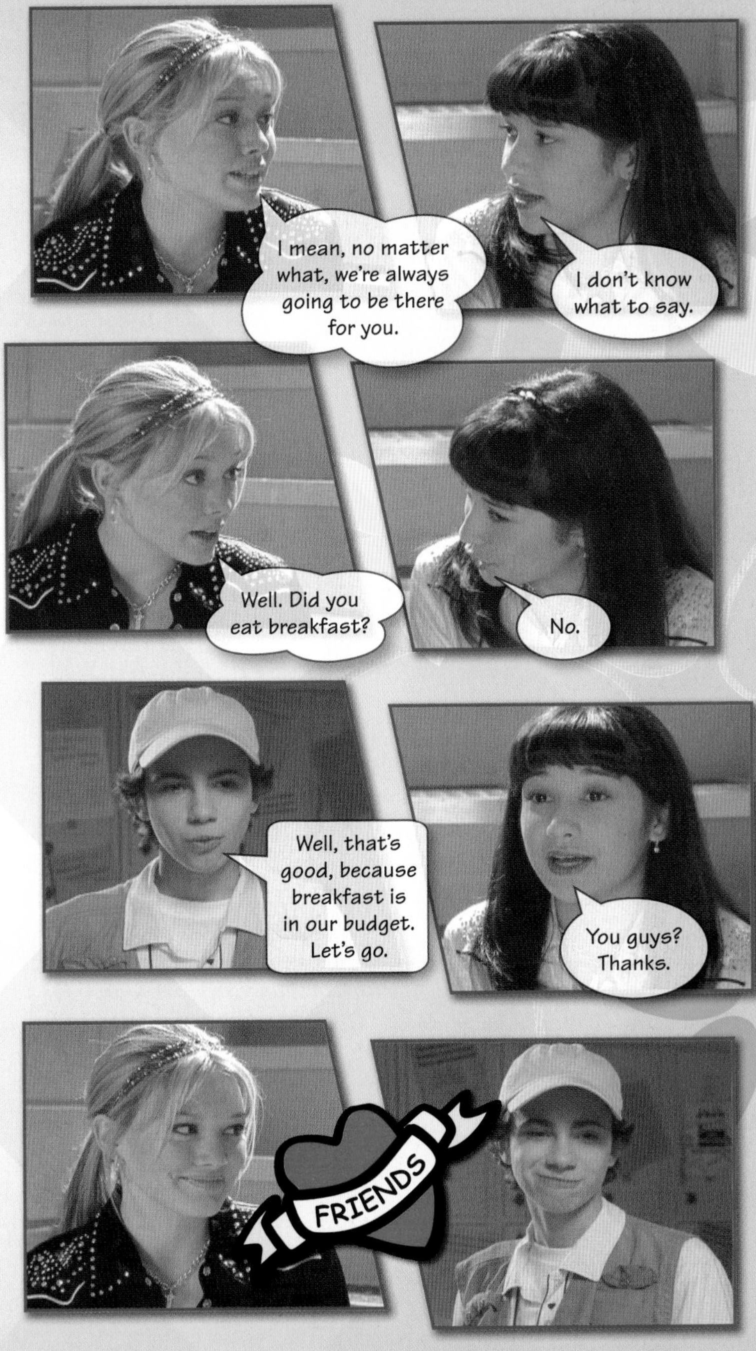

I mean, no matter what, we're always going to be there for you.
I don't know what to say.
Well. Did you eat breakfast?
No.
Well, that's good, because breakfast is in our budget. Let's go.
You guys? Thanks.
FRIENDS

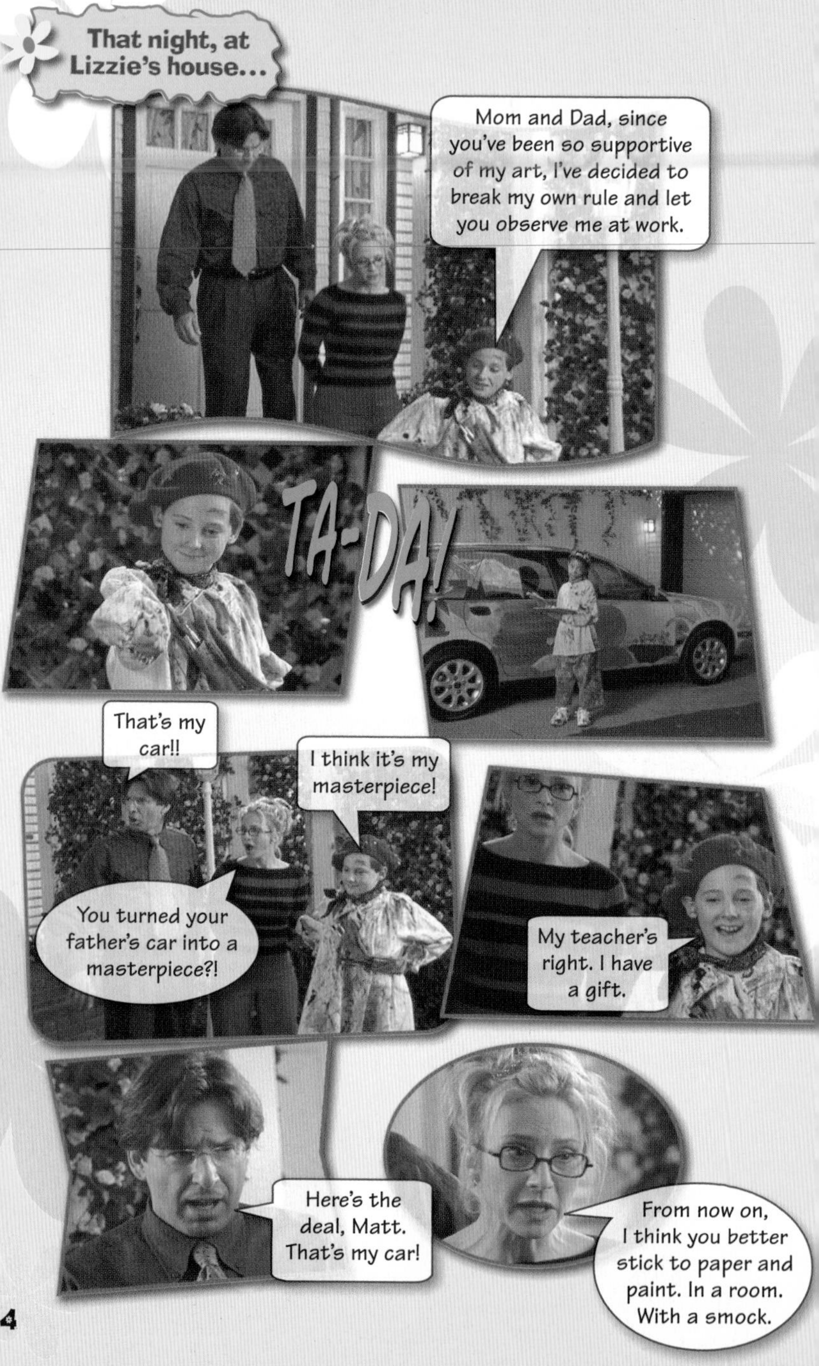
That night, at Lizzie's house...
Mom and Dad, since you've been so supportive of my art, I've decided to break my own rule and let you observe me at work.
TA-DA!
That's my car!!
I think it's my masterpiece!
You turned your father's car into a masterpiece?!
My teacher's right. I have a gift.
Here's the deal, Matt. That's my car!
From now on, I think you better stick to paper and paint. In a room. With a smock.

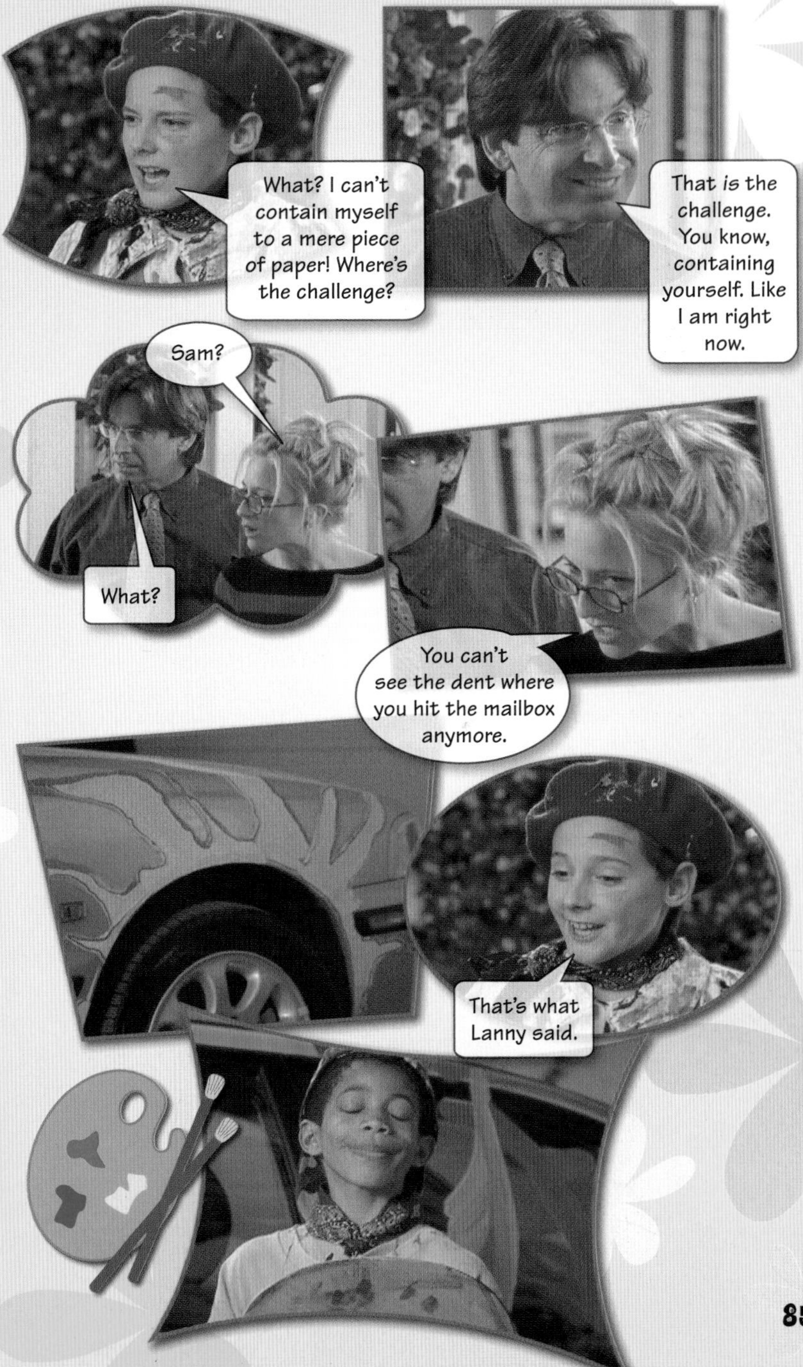
What? I can't contain myself to a mere piece of paper! Where's the challenge?
That *is* the challenge. You know, containing yourself. Like I am right now.
Sam?
What?
You can't see the dent where you hit the mailbox anymore.
That's what Lanny said.

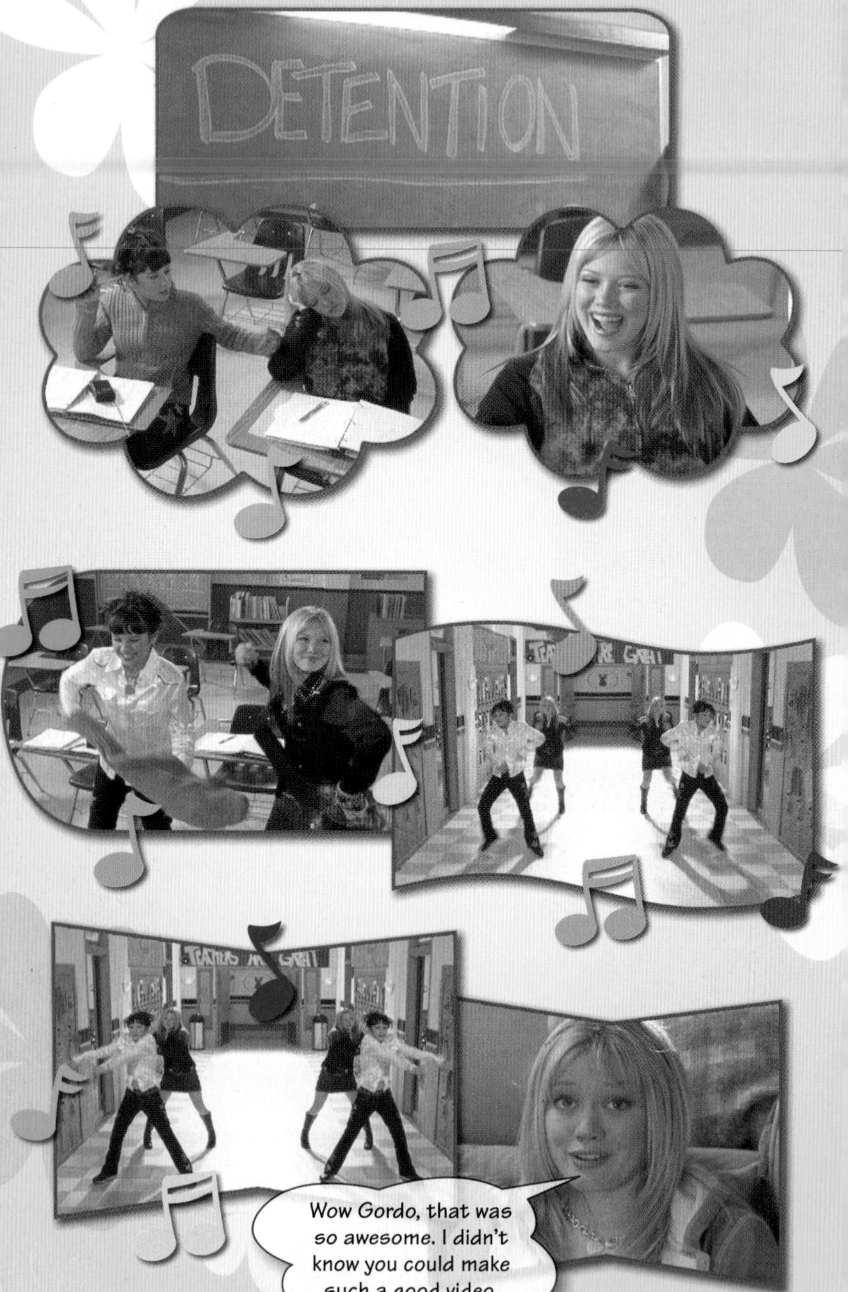
DETENTION
Wow Gordo, that was so awesome. I didn't know you could make such a good video.

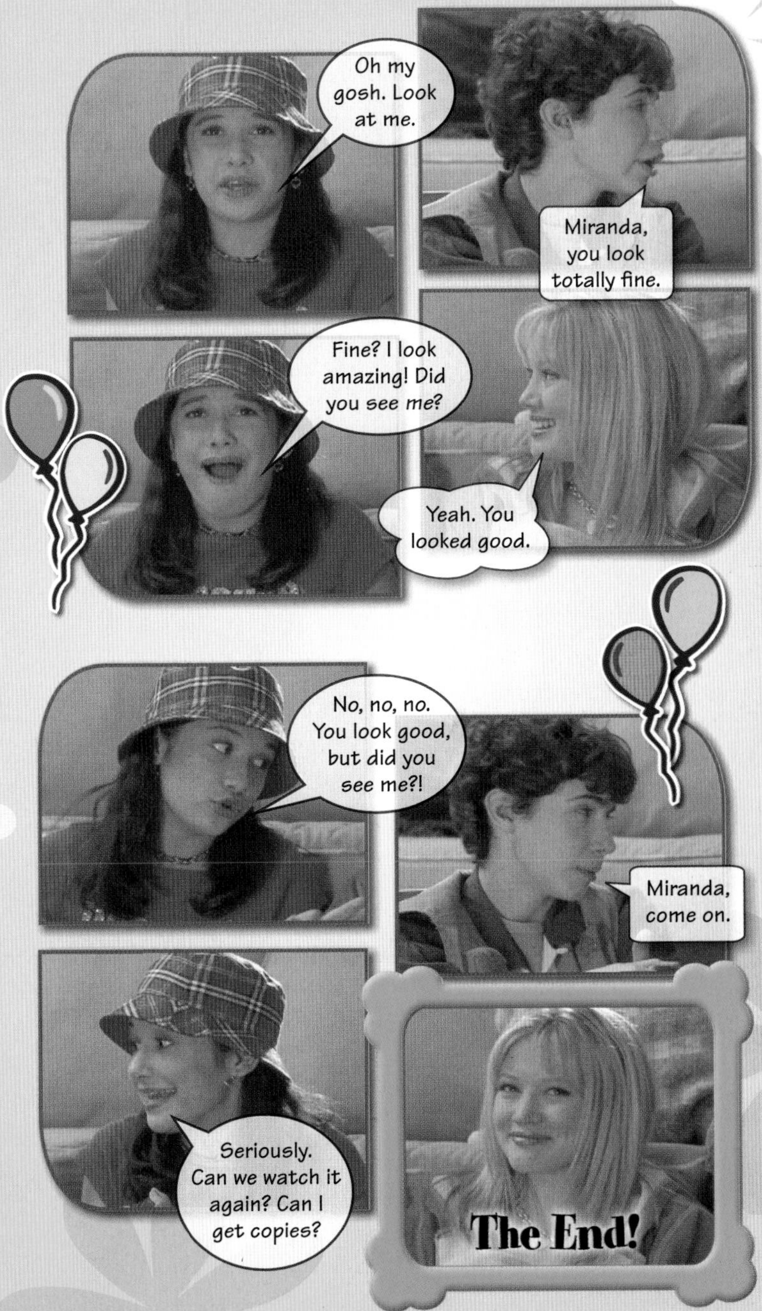

Oh my gosh. Look at me.
Miranda, you look totally fine.
Fine? I look amazing! Did you see me?
Yeah. You looked good.
No, no, no. You look good, but did you see me?!
Miranda, come on.
Seriously. Can we watch it again? Can I get copies?
The End!

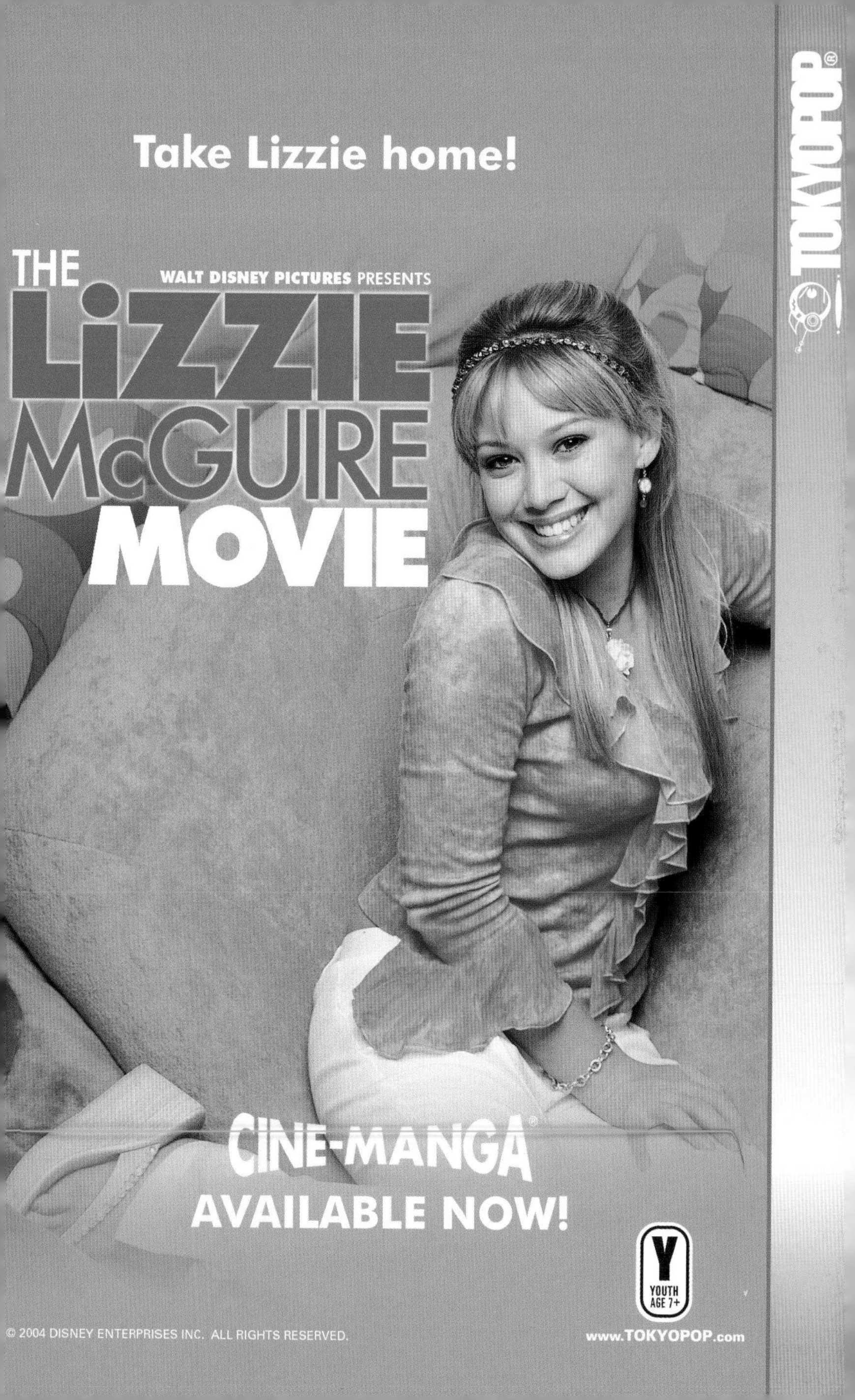
Take Lizzie home!
WALT DISNEY PICTURES PRESENTS
THE LiZZIE McGUIRE MOVIE
CINE-MANGA®
AVAILABLE NOW!
Y
YOUTH AGE 7+
© 2004 DISNEY ENTERPRISES INC. ALL RIGHTS RESERVED.
www.TOKYOPOP.com
TOKYOPOP®

MANGA

.HACK//LEGEND OF THE TWILIGHT
ANGELIC LAYER
BABY BIRTH
BRAIN POWERED
BRIGADOON
B'TX
CANDIDATE FOR GODDESS, THE
CARDCAPTOR SAKURA
CARDCAPTOR SAKURA - MASTER OF THE CLOW
CHRONICLES OF THE CURSED SWORD
CLAMP SCHOOL DETECTIVES
CLOVER
COMIC PARTY
CORRECTOR YUI
COWBOY BEBOP
COWBOY BEBOP: SHOOTING STAR
CRESCENT MOON
CROSS
CULDCEPT
CYBORG 009
D•N•ANGEL
DEMON DIARY
DEMON ORORON, THE
DIGIMON
DIGIMON TAMERS
DIGIMON ZERO TWO
DRAGON HUNTER
DRAGON KNIGHTS
DRAGON VOICE
DREAM SAGA
DUKLYON: CLAMP SCHOOL DEFENDERS
ET CETERA
ETERNITY
FAERIES' LANDING
FLCL
FLOWER OF THE DEEP SLEEP, THE
FORBIDDEN DANCE
FRUITS BASKET
G GUNDAM
GATEKEEPERS
GIRL GOT GAME
GUNDAM SEED ASTRAY
GUNDAM WING
GUNDAM WING: BATTLEFIELD OF PACIFISTS
GUNDAM WING: ENDLESS WALTZ
GUNDAM WING: THE LAST OUTPOST (G-UNIT)
HANDS OFF!
HARLEM BEAT

HYPER RUNE
I.N.V.U.
INITIAL D
INSTANT TEEN: JUST ADD NUTS
JING: KING OF BANDITS
JING: KING OF BANDITS - TWILIGHT TALES
JULINE
KARE KANO
KILL ME, KISS ME
KINDAICHI CASE FILES, THE
KING OF HELL
KODOCHA: SANA'S STAGE
LEGEND OF CHUN HYANG, THE
LOVE OR MONEY
MAGIC KNIGHT RAYEARTH I
MAGIC KNIGHT RAYEARTH II
MAN OF MANY FACES
MARMALADE BOY
MARS
MARS: HORSE WITH NO NAME
MINK
MIRACLE GIRLS
MODEL
MOURYOU KIDEN: LEGEND OF THE NYMPHS
NECK AND NECK
ONE
ONE I LOVE, THE
PEACH GIRL
PEACH GIRL: CHANGE OF HEART
PITA-TEN
PLANET LADDER
PLANETES
PRESIDENT DAD
PRINCESS AI
PSYCHIC ACADEMY
QUEEN'S KNIGHT, THE
RAGNAROK
RAVE MASTER
REALITY CHECK
REBIRTH
REBOUND
RISING STARS OF MANGA
SAILOR MOON
SAINT TAIL
SAMURAI GIRL REAL BOUT HIGH SCHOOL
SEIKAI TRILOGY, THE
SGT. FROG
SHAOLIN SISTERS
SHIRAHIME-SYO: SNOW GODDESS TALES

07.15.04Y

ALSO AVAILABLE FROM TOKYOPOP®

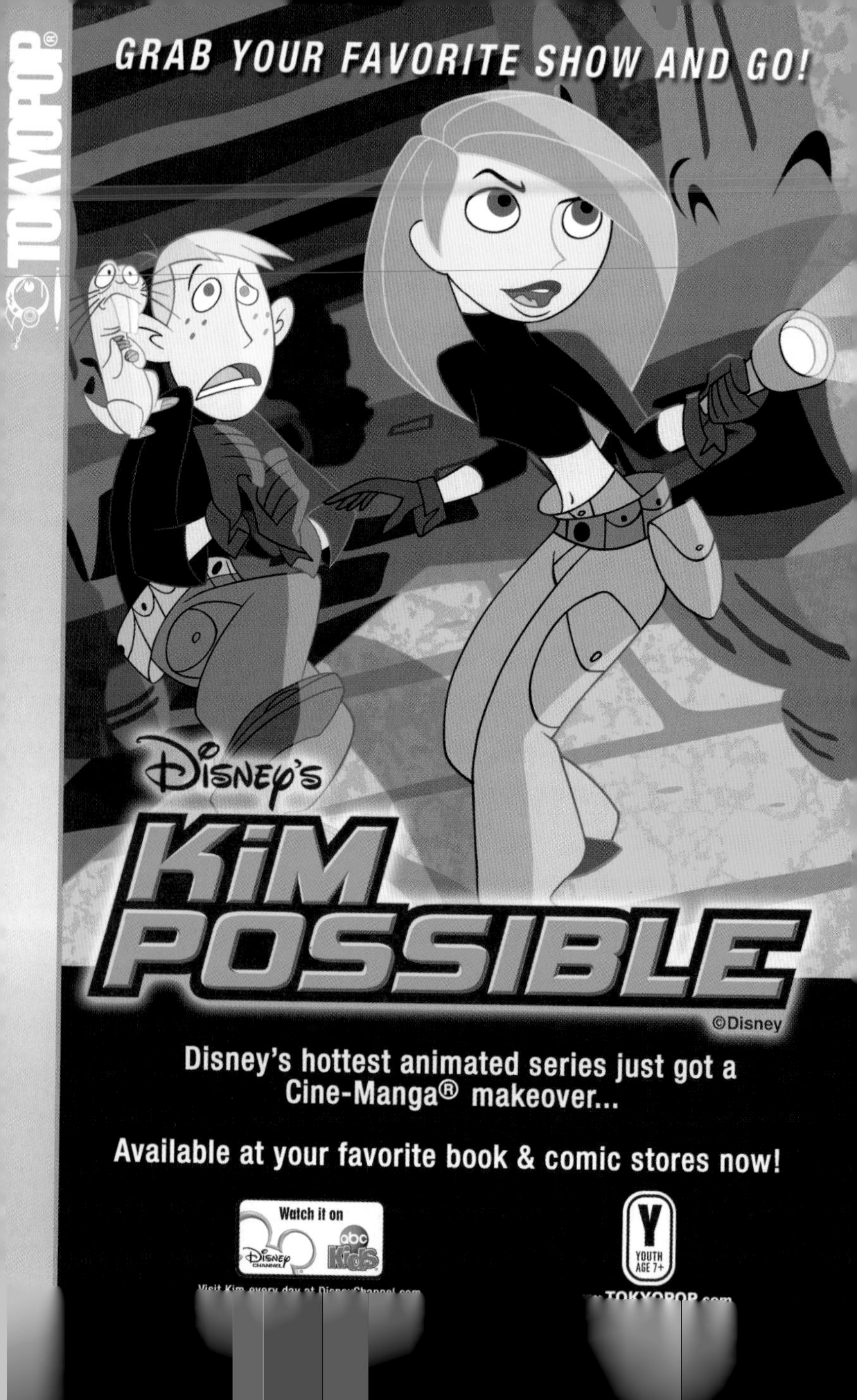
TOKYOPOP
GRAB YOUR FAVORITE SHOW AND GO!
Disney's
Kim Possible
©Disney
Disney's hottest animated series just got a Cine-Manga® makeover...
Available at your favorite book & comic stores now!
Watch it on
Disney Channel
abc Kids
Y
YOUTH AGE 7+

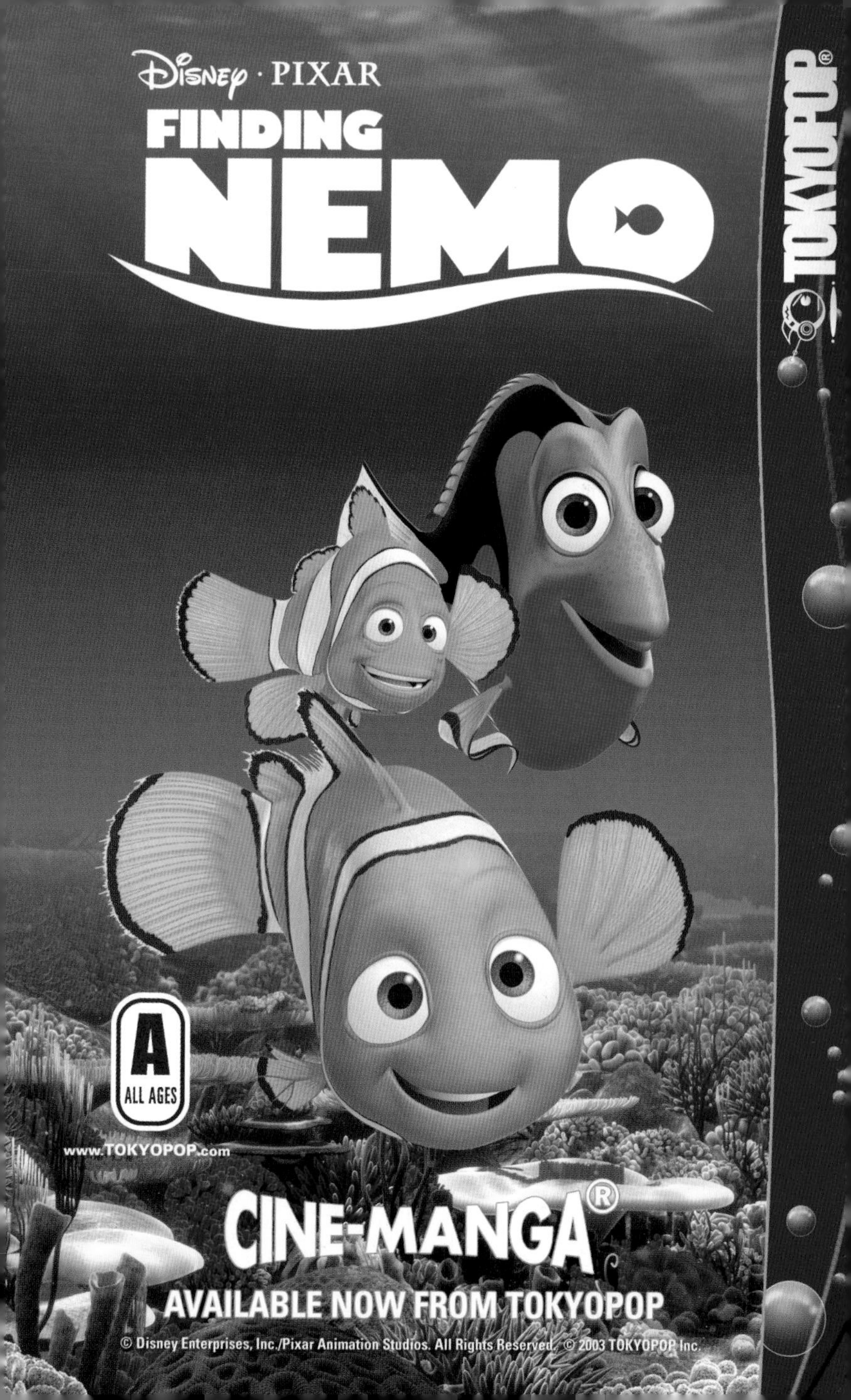
Disney · PIXAR
FINDING NEMO
TOKYOPOP
A ALL AGES
www.TOKYOPOP.com
CINE-MANGA®
AVAILABLE NOW FROM TOKYOPOP
© Disney Enterprises, Inc./Pixar Animation Studios. All Rights Reserved. © 2003 TOKYOPOP Inc.

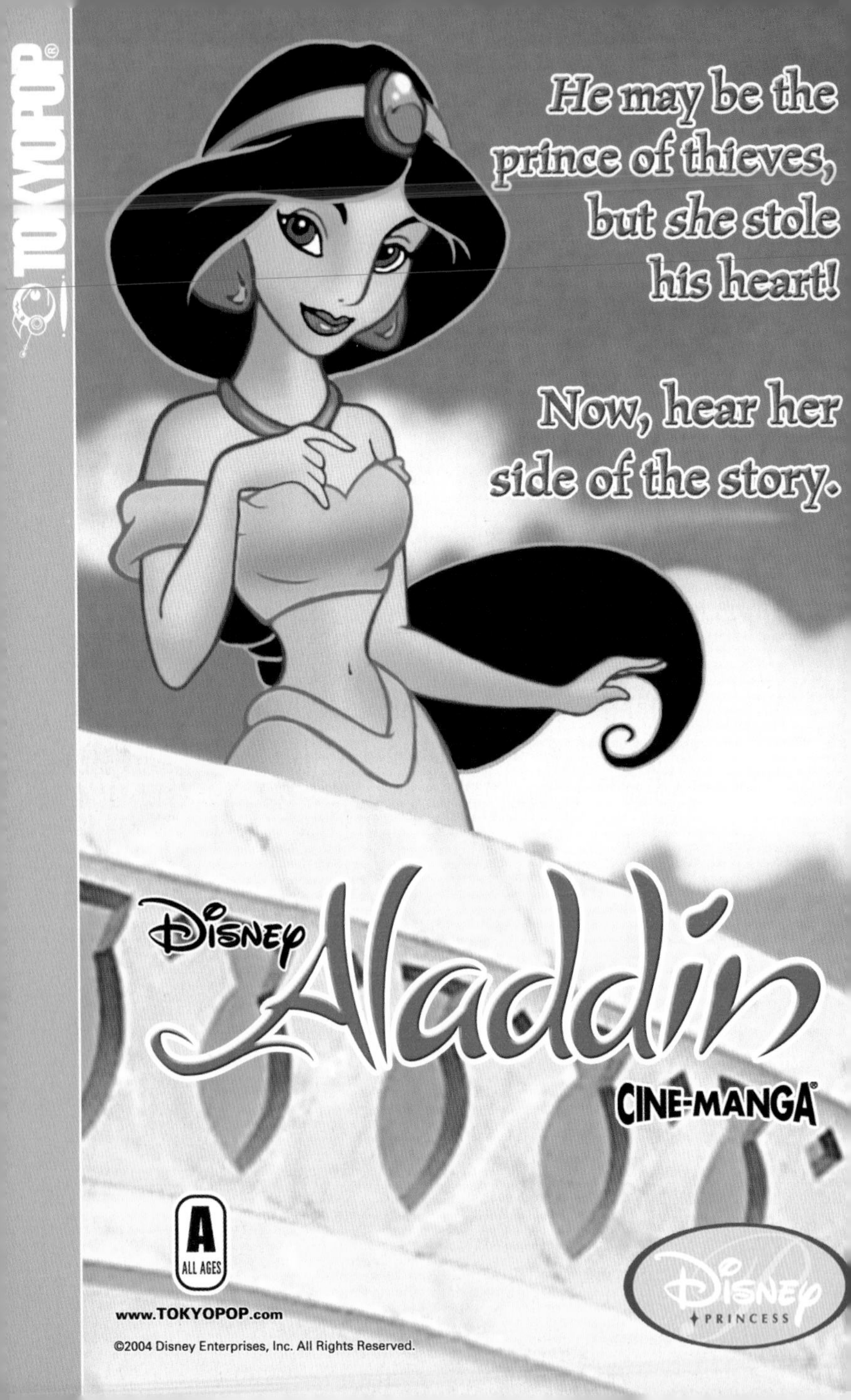
TOKYOPOP
He may be the prince of thieves, but she stole his heart!
Now, hear her side of the story.
Disney Aladdin
CINE-MANGA
A ALL AGES
www.TOKYOPOP.com
©2004 Disney Enterprises, Inc. All Rights Reserved.
Disney PRINCESS

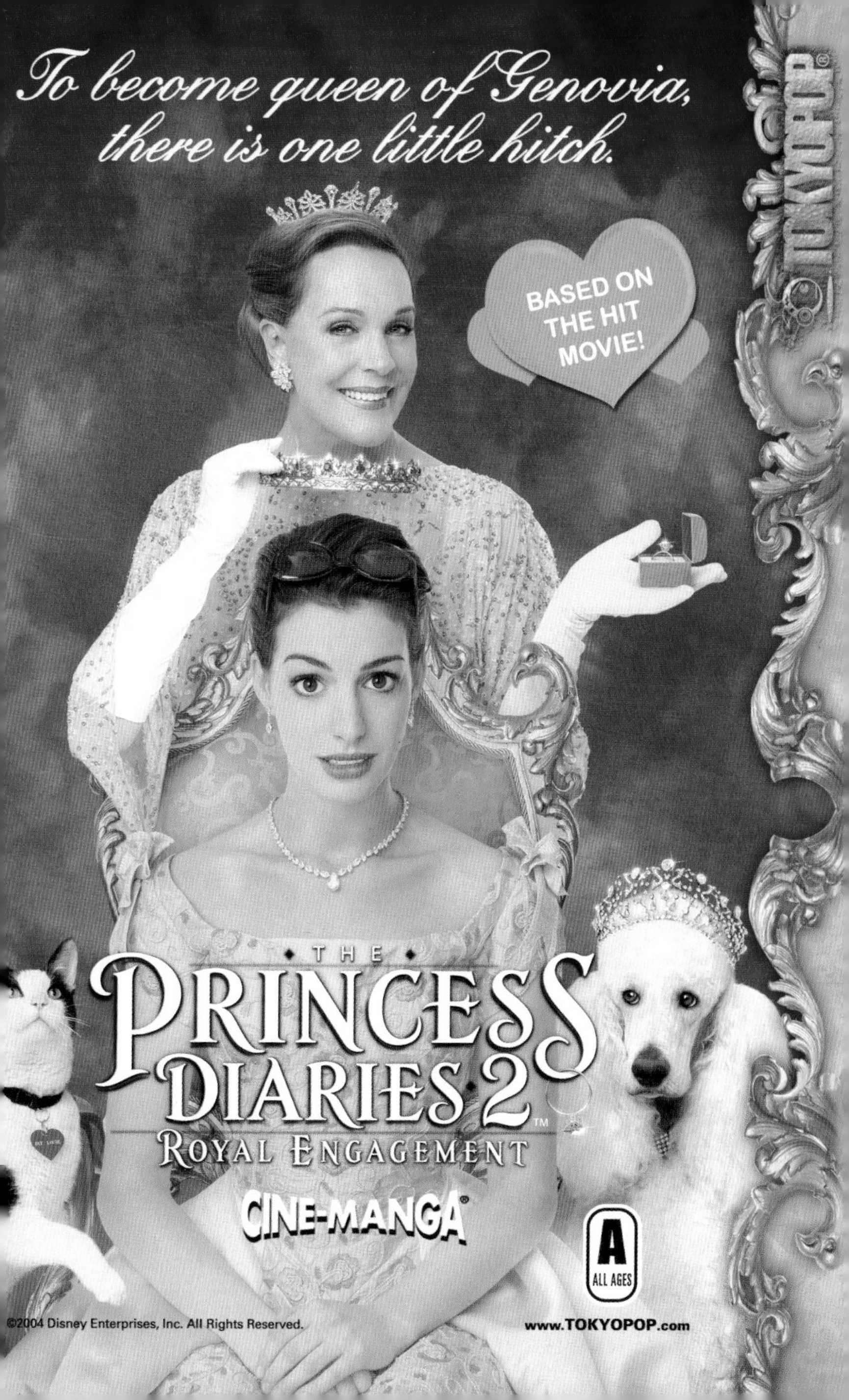
To become queen of Genovia, there is one little hitch.
TOKYOPOP®
BASED ON THE HIT MOVIE!
THE PRINCESS DIARIES 2™
ROYAL ENGAGEMENT
CINE-MANGA®
A ALL AGES
©2004 Disney Enterprises, Inc. All Rights Reserved.
www.TOKYOPOP.com

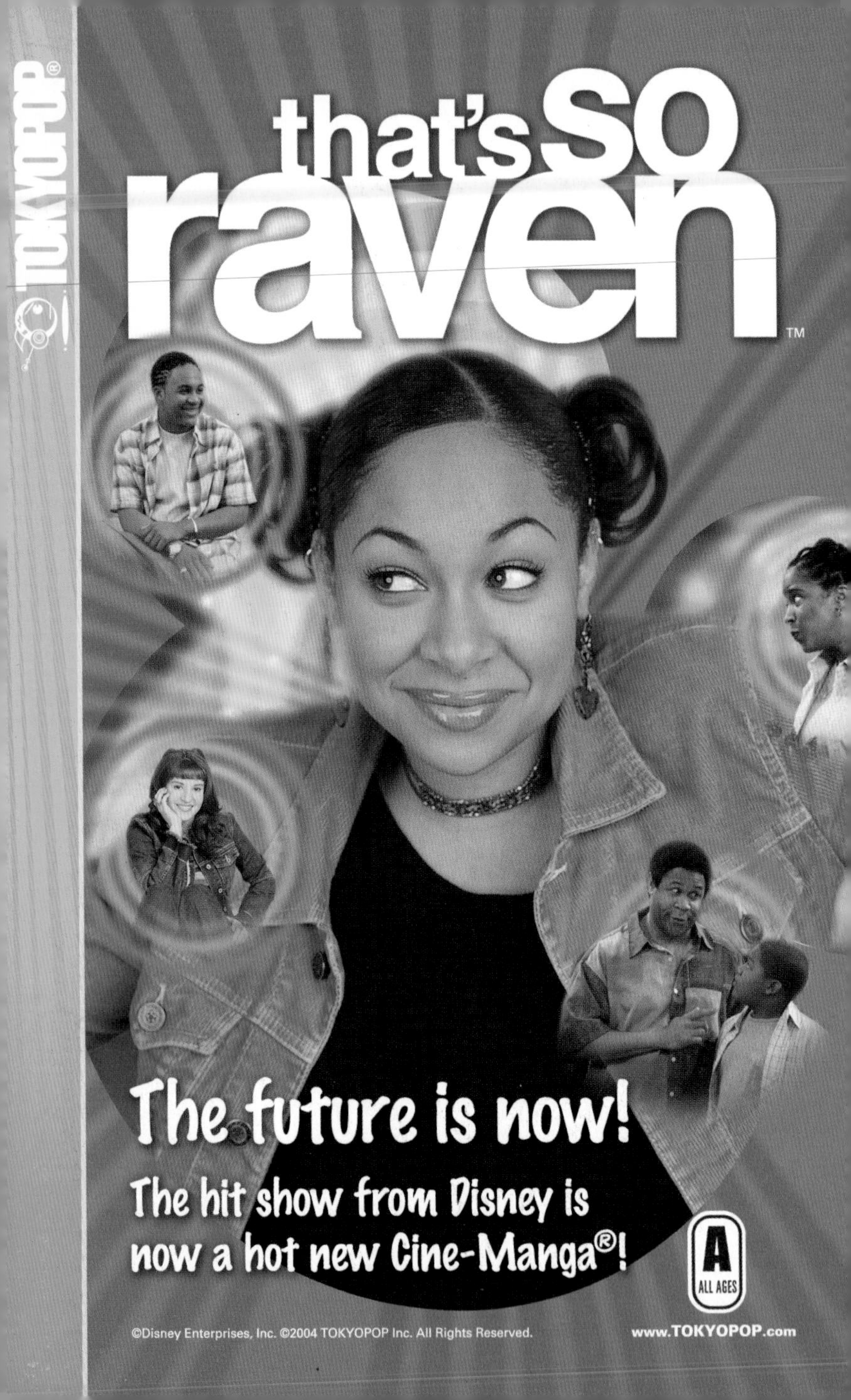
TOKYOPOP®
that's SO raven™
The future is now!
The hit show from Disney is now a hot new Cine-Manga®!
A ALL AGES
©Disney Enterprises, Inc. ©2004 TOKYOPOP Inc. All Rights Reserved.
www.TOKYOPOP.com